A New Gu

A New Guide
to the
Debate about God

Martin Prozesky

SCM PRESS LTD

ISBN 0 334 01123 X

First published 1992 by
SCM Press Ltd
26–30 Tottenham Road London N1 4BZ

Phototypeset by Intype, London
Printed in Great Britain by
Mackays of Chatham, Kent

Contents

1   The God Question Today   1

2   The Case for the Believer   19

3   The Case against the Believer   78

4   Judging the Debate   131

Select Bibliography   175

Index   179

Acknowledgments

My work on this book was aided by various people whose assistance I gratefully acknowledge: Dr John Thresher for making it possible for me to discuss aspects of chapter 3 with staff members at the European Centre for Nuclear Research near Geneva, and for subsequently checking my account of those discussions; also his colleagues Dr John Ellis and Dr Andrei Linde, now at Stanford University, for various clarifications and suggestions; colleagues at the University of Natal for helpfully commenting on and where necessary correcting various scientific points in chapter 2, namely Professors Roger Raab and Paul Jackson of the Department of Physics, and Professor Gordon MacLean of the Department of Zoology; and my departmental colleagues in Philosophy and Religious Studies at the same university, namely Patrick Maxwell, Simon Beck and Ronald Nicolson, for making a number of helpful suggestions for which I am also most grateful. I must also thank the University of Natal for the study leave during which part of this book was researched and written. Lastly, I am once again deeply indebted to my wife Elizabeth for her critical insights, patience and encouragement throughout the writing of this book, and to our sons Justin and David for helping me keep my prose from being too academic.

The God Question Today

It is noon on a sun-filled September day in Rome and the church bells are ringing. My view from the Palatine Hill stretches from the Colosseum where Christians once went to the lions, to the Victor Emmanuel Memorial and the Senate away to my left. Beyond them but out of sight across the Tiber stands the Vatican, heartland of the world's biggest single religious body, the Roman Catholic Church. It is impossible to miss the signs of Christianity's power, and I find myself moved by the memory of a crucified carpenter's message, spoken long ago and far away, prevailing over the lions and the Caesars and the established faiths amidst which it here took root.

Below me lie the ruins of Imperial Rome, the Rome of the Caesars and their gods, of Jupiter and Venus and Vesta, the city of Marcus Aurelius, the philosopher king, and of Nero who was king but no philosopher. Straight ahead is the Basilica of Maxentius, or at least what remains of it. As I hear the bells of Christian Rome, what I see is the graveyard of an older Rome where the ancient gods once filled the Roman soul, a graveyard where lizards and grass and visitors like me now hold sway. Above us a jet airliner climbs into the skies, reminding me of the newest Rome of all, the Rome of technology, electronics and mass global travel, and I find myself wondering, despite the signs of triumph all around me, whether the Christian religion as we have known it is perhaps also headed for its own graveyard, whether it too has reached its own high noon?

This is a good question to ask anywhere in the world, but especially in Rome where the life and death of entire religions can be seen so strikingly if you know where to look. I could see it that September day, see it in the way Christian churches had been built around the older pagan temples they displaced, see it in the way Christian crosses had been placed on top of ancient Egyptian obelisks, themselves plundered by Jupiter-worshipping Caesars from an even older faith that once thrived beside the Nile in my native Africa but which now endures only in pyramids and mummies. Is that what lies ahead for the faith that once shed its blood in the Colosseum? Judging by the thousands who flock to see Christian Rome, this hardly seems possible, till you notice that it is art and architecture that lure them there as much as faith, for there are often many more people present on a weekday gazing at Michelangelo than attending Mass on Sunday.

The heart of the Catholic Church may be Rome, but the heart of the Christian faith is its belief in the God it says has been made uniquely and physically real by Jesus of Nazareth. The Christianity we have inherited and whose bells were ringing that September day in Rome stands or falls with the soundness of that faith in God. I have read and heard thousands of words about the deity whom Christians worship, but none struck me as deeply as a short sentence with which David Jenkins, Bishop of Durham, began his book *Living with Questions*. He wrote, 'God is either a gift or a delusion.' There are of course many millions of Christians all over the world who testify that the greatest gift in their lives is indeed the God they find in and through Jesus Christ, describing him as the source of all goodness, truth, beauty and joy, and the world's only hope for the future. But there are also millions who think otherwise, sensing here a massive delusion which stands in the way of human maturity and well-being. This book is about the debate between these two great groups. Because that debate affects us all and not just academic specialists, I have presented it in this book in such a way that general readers can easily follow the various arguments and reach their own rational conclusions.

The central questions I shall be posing are therefore as follows: how sound is belief in God as taught by the historic Christian churches? Will the kind of people we would admire most and whom the world truly needs believe that there is in fact such a God or not – people who sincerely seek the truth by facing all the relevant evidence, weighing it sensitively, critically and fairly, and who care deeply for the well-being of all? Does faith in God continue to thrive because it wins the respect of such people, or is it living off – and eroding – the inherited capital of the past? As will be clear from these questions, it is *Christianity's* belief in God that is at issue in this book, not the other great God-orientated religions like Islam, Hinduism or Judaism. They are drawn into the discussion as significant parts of that large majority of the world's people which disagrees with Christianity or rejects it outright. The rationality of their belief in a God is a separate matter which is not at issue here.

Reasons for a new look at the debate about God

Why raise such questions at a time when Christianity seems to be enjoying a new bouyancy, when the Christian West has so clearly won the contest with the atheistic Marxist world? The reasons are that despite that buoyancy, the debate about God in the Christian world is a debate which needs to be handled much more comprehensively than in the past, and it is a debate whose time has now come because we are living in a period of great global need and scope for taking stock of our entire heritage, including our inherited religious beliefs. Let me explain.

To start with, faith in God – or 'theism', as it is also called – is by no means as secure as many believers think. In the wider context of religious and philosophical thought outside the churches it is, in fact, a widely disputed and often rejected idea. Many who dispute and reject it are themselves people of the highest moral, spiritual and intellectual calibre, so that their doubts can't be dismissed as trivial or malicious. But seldom do we find those doubts adequately considered by believers. On the other hand, few atheists and agnostics give serious attention to the best kind of argument in favour of the believer, preferring to attack and reject feeble or outdated versions of the believer's case which no serious theist would offer today. As a result, neither side hears its opponents' best arguments.

There is a further problem. So far the debate has been very provincial. People forget (or ignore) the great importance of the other religions of the world, and proceed as if there were only two contending voices – Christian believers in God and Western-style non-believers. It is high time we overcame such an insular outlook and thought in more global terms. In this book we will therefore set up a debate between Christian believers on the one hand and all their main critics on the other. Among those critics the most vocal and radical are certainly the secular-minded Westerners I alluded to above, with their belief that the physical universe is the only reality and that all religion is false, so I shall pay greatest attention to their attacks on theism. But Christianity has other critics as well, other God-believing people like Jews, Muslims and many Hindus, people from religions like Taoism and Buddhism which find the concept of God religiously unnecessary, and – importantly – members and supporters of the women's movement in the West, many of them Christians. It is extremely significant that many women, including large numbers who remain loyal to the churches – find the prevailing Christian concept of God false and dehumanizing. Their voices will therefore also be heard in this book.

There is also a pressing practical reason for exploring this problem. Maybe we are approaching the last century of life on this planet because of pollution. But even if we survive the environmental crisis there are other serious problems to face, like hunger, injustice and tyranny. These also exist on a scale never before experienced. Ours is a world in pain; a world made ugly by evils of our own making; perhaps even a world under sentence of death. But although humanity may be placing itself on death row, the paradox is that vast numbers of people at the same time are crying out against this madness. Amidst the starvation, exploitation, wars and pollution, amidst the greed, cruelty and indifference that fuel these evils, there are also millions who long to help the earth and the fragile film of life that covers it.

Theirs is a dream that will not go away until our present crisis has been solved. They have glimpsed something with the power to overcome all other ideas : a vision of the greatest well-being for all, a world where everybody has a stake in the fulfilment of everybody else because nothing else has better prospects of creating lasting peace and plenty for all of us. Some of us see this vision of attainable planetary well-being as a new breakthrough of human consciousness in relation to which everything else in our late twentieth-century culture will have to be evaluated and changed.

4

Amidst this global situation the world needs all the saving energies, all the saving wisdom we can summon. Every sector of life must play its part here by taking a hard look at itself and changing whatever harms humanity and our planet. The business people must do so in their sector. Politicians, the media people, educationists, lawyers and all others must do so in theirs and in dialogue with one another. And the same applies to religion, above all to the Christians of the world because of their vast numbers and historic links with the rise of capitalism and colonialism. They too must take stock, asking just as searchingly what their world-view, values and deeds have contributed to the world's problems.

As well as this need for stock-taking, the world presently has a rare chance to carry it out. The collapse of the old communist order in Eastern Europe has effectively freed us of the defensive stance of the cold war period. No longer is there a God-believing West confronted by an atheistic Eastern bloc of nations. The state-backed atheism of the old Moscow and its satellites is dead and gone, and the cathedral bells are ringing again in Red Square. But that must not mislead us into thinking that all is well in the West, religiously or otherwise. The real position is that we are now free to turn a much-needed spotlight upon ourselves and our own shortcomings in order to make whatever changes we need to build a better world.

The old situation was strongly polarized and confrontational. This fostered a great deal of unconscious dogmatism as each side firmed up what it regarded as its own contradictory essentials – dogmatic atheism in Red Square and an equally unyielding theism in St Peter's Square or amongst Bible-believing Christians. Amidst confrontation and dogma there is little scope for self-criticality and debate; but when they recede or are overcome there is plenty and we would be foolish to ignore the historic possibilities that are now open to us. After all, as Epicurus reportedly said, 'The impious person is not the person who rejects the gods of the multitude, but who adheres to the conception the multitude has of the gods.'

This is even more necessary when we look further eastward, beyond the former USSR, to the countries of the Pacific Rim. Theirs is the real economic miracle of our time, yet those countries have never had the kind of God-centred world-view we know in the West.

Is there a message here for the world's Christians and their confident faith that God alone is the source of all good and that faith in him is the only sure way to his blessings? We need to face that question, Americans perhaps more so than any others because they are overwhelmingly Christian in orientation and no longer in sole command of the economic (or moral) high ground of the world.

For a South African like me there is added pressure to look again at the debate about God. South Africa is far from the global centres of industrial and political power, though it has seldom been far from the the world's moral outrage over the past few decades. Its population is relatively small, its situation remote. But in one respect South Africa is arguably at the centre of things: the relevance of Christianity to good and evil in human existence. In South Africa we have seen a most vicious kind of inhumanity built into a whole way of life in the form of apartheid. Here evil has been grimly real, sometimes in obvious ways but also in deceptively subtle and plausible ways, for example when it masquerades as the voice of God. Yet few countries have been as strongly affected by Christianity as South Africa, with over 90% of its whites and most blacks regarding themselves as Christians. In South Africa there has thus been a unique, side-by-side thriving of Christian faith in God as the source of all goodness, and the evils of apartheid. This forces us to ask how that could ever have happened if God really is the most powerful force of all, especially for people who have opened their lives to him and his goodness.

My next reason for exploring this debate is to test the very buoyancy among many Christians that was mentioned earlier in this chapter, for example their sense that modern physics is now firmly on their side. Let me illustrate. Referring to the picture modern physics gives us of nature, a well-known theologian has written that nature points to the presence of intention. In other words, it reveals a divine creator. These words are not from a twice-born fundamentalist in the American Bible-belt. Nor are they a piece of obsolete piety from the Middle Ages. They are the verdict of a sophisticated, contemporary Cambridge theologian. If he is correct then particle physics is today's ally for believers in God, and quarks will have replaced question-marks in the minds of the faithful. Nor is this theologian a solo voice; on the contrary, there is a whole choir of Christian believers singing the same confident song.

But are they right? Have they really looked hard enough at this ancient but still thriving notion, the notion that absolutely everything has come into being through the creative action of a God? I do not think so, and intend therefore to remedy that shortcoming so far as I can in this book by taking a deeper look at the foundations on which Christianity claims to stand, its distinctive concept of God. I shall do so, partly, by using insights and responses obtained from experts in particle physics during a visit to the Mecca of that kind of modern science, the international nuclear research centre called CERN outside Geneva, coupled with insights drawn from atheistic and secular humanist sources and from the other great religions of the world. In this way a much fuller debate about God can be conducted than the ones we have hitherto heard.

A further reason for writing a new guide to the debate about God is therefore a conviction that existing discussions of this topic, valuable though they all are in their own ways, leave out too many important issues. David Jenkins himself wrote a short *Guide to the Debate About God* thirty years ago which is stimulating and full of insight, but it deals only with the debate among Christian theologians about the *nature* of God. In this book I explore a different topic, namely the *existence* of God, with Christian ideas making up only one side of the debate. Next, I find that most Christian writers overestimate the strength of their side of the argument and under-rate the opposition. In particular, I think they seriously underestimate the challenges posed to Christian theism by secular experience, by non-theistic religions, by natural evil and by moral objections to Christianity. On the other hand, I have yet to find a Western-style sceptic who does justice to the strengths of the Christian case for faith in God. Above all I miss a book which brings the two sides of the debate together in a concise but comprehensive way. This book has been designed to help overcome these problems.

The last reason for writing this book is more personal. In recent years I have read with great interest the arguments of Don Cupitt and others who find fault with Christian theism, as well as the rejoinders of those who think it is still valid. One day not long ago, after reflecting on these things and especially on the problems brought to light by those who reject theism, it suddenly occurred to me that instead of these criticisms being a sign that the concept of God was on its death-bed, as the critics say, could it not be that theism is only now leaving its childhood? If so, then God-orientated religion would today be in much the same situation as science between Copernicus and Galileo: much in need of a new transformation, but still essentially pointing in the right direction. In that case it would need criticism, modification and enrichment, not rejection. One of the aims of this book is to test that possibility.

Our true nature as human beings

As well as being about God, this book is also about us as humans because our true identity is tied up with the God-question. Are we in fact the children of a Creator God? Or of a purely natural cosmos? Or of something else as yet undreamt of in either cathedral or physics laboratory? On the answer depends much more than we might think. The God-question affects the roots of our self-understanding, making it no mere academic debate between Cambridge clerics and Stanford scientists. It affects us in some highly practical ways. Many Jews and Christians, for instance, think that God gave Israel the right to the Holy Land – but a billion Muslims think that God did no such thing. Desmond Tutu and many others believe that God is on the side of the oppressed. Oppressive governments disagree – and slash welfare spending accordingly. In America the God-question affects state and federal politics, for example in campaigns against the theory of evolution or in demands for and against prayers in public schools. In South Africa we have had some leading white Christians demanding to hear from Nelson Mandela where he stands in relation to Christianity, evidently implying that only Christian believers in God can make good leaders – a disturbing notion anywhere but especially so when we recall that the man who launched the apartheid state in 1948 was not just a Christian but an ordained minister who moved from his church into politics as a believing Christian.

For the good of humanity everywhere we therefore need a fresh look at theism, and as we survey the God-question we need to remember that not a single public prayer or bent knee, not a line of God-based legislation or moralizing from womb to tomb is justified if the case for God is not at least as strong as the case against. And the same is true in reverse.

The methods used in this book

In what follows I shall try to portray the Christian idea and experience of God, the arguments given by believers in defence of their faith and the objections raised against them as fairly, accurately and attractively as possible. It is easy to set up a caricature and then demolish it. Some sceptics fall into that trap but victory over a hobbled opponent is no victory at all. Certainly this is no way to establish truth. But without the truth nothing can really prosper, so we need the best way to discover it in connection with the debate about God.

To my mind the way forward is to let each side state its case as fully, persuasively and validly as possible, and then weigh the various arguments according to agreed methods of judgment. On the basis of this policy I have made a point of immersing myself in the arguments of both Christian believers and their critics in order to portray their arguments as strongly as I can, ignoring the sometimes feeble ploys both sides occasionally use, like simplistic appeals to biblical authority or sceptics who rely more on scorn than argument.

On the basis of this policy of listening carefully to both sides, there are three chapters after the present one. The first two contain the arguments in favour of and against Christian theism. Each is approached with the same willingness to hear the two sets of debaters at their most effective, and the dispute between them is judged in the final chapter by norms accepted by both sides, which I will explain later in this chapter.

As we enter this fascinating debate let us remember that if believers are right about God, then it is an infinitely vast and mysterious being whom we will be considering in this book, whereas our own mental powers are limited. Equally, let us never lose sight of the vastness and mystery of nature, many of whose secrets still lie hidden from even the best human mind, so that all our theories about the universe are based on incomplete knowledge. Science, in other words, has by no means reached the end of its role, just as we humans can have no God's-eye view of things. Certainly we must think critically and have faith in our ability to solve problems but without over-estimating those powers. Instead, ours must be the more realistic goal of discovering all we can by using our minds to the full, while firmly denying a doorway to dogmatism in our own minds. The quest explored in this book is by limited humans for the most probable answers to a very big question amidst a vastly complex and mysterious cosmos. In such a context wise enquirers protect themselves against error by submitting belief to criticism on the basis of appropriate criteria applied fairly to comprehensive, accurate evidence. This is not infallible but it is the best we can do. Belief itself does not seem to be something we can change at will, except where the evidence is very evenly balanced. For example, I find that I cannot simply decide by an act of will to stop believing that a free press is desirable. For me to change my beliefs about that would require a great deal of very strong evidence indeed, and not an act of will by me. But we can choose to live by a policy of actively seeking the best evidence and testing our convictions and those of others, rather than holding or dismissing them ignorantly, dogmatically or uncritically.

This book is written on the basis of that policy. It is directed primarily at the large number of fairminded people who share the same outlook. Studies of our thinking skills by experts like Piaget, Erikson and Kohlberg show that there are stages of mental and moral development and that open-minded criticality in relation to different world-views is something we have to learn. Similarly, Fowler has identified six stages of faith, not all of which are reached. Three of them occur typically during childhood and adolescence. They are marked by imitation, literalism and conformity. Some people remain there for life. Criticality, on the other hand, only comes as a fourth stage well into adult life for most who acquire it. At the relatively rare fifth stage some people learn to be 'open to the strange truth of others', as Ruth Tiffany Barnhouse puts it. Rarer still is Fowler's sixth stage where faith creatively takes a truly universal and inclusive form. In terms of these psychological theories the debate explored in the present book requires stage four and five skills, and is thus accessible to any thoughtful reader who has ever wondered where the truth really lies concerning things like the different faiths and philosophies and our own human destiny (if any), or who has sensed the force of beliefs other than his or her own.

As for the criteria for judging the various arguments, these must be fair to both sides. To meet this requirement I have taken them from both religious and secular thinkers, though I first found them being recommended by the evangelical Christian writer Arthur Holmes in his book *All Truth is God's Truth*. The first one is that the beliefs in question be *clear*, so that we know what we are being asked to accept; next, that any supposed facts associated with them be supported by the best *evidence*, especially evidence which people can check for themselves; and thirdly that all arguments offered by the disputing parties be *logically coherent and valid*. Let us look a bit more fully into these three criteria.

Firstly, the concept of God and anything proposed instead of it must be clearly and coherently stated. If this doesn't happen then the debate won't even get off the ground, either because we will not know what we are talking about or because nothing in reality can ever correspond to an incoherent idea. For example, square circles and married bachelors are incoherent ideas. What they name cannot possibly exist because the first half of the idea is totally cancelled by the second.

At this first hurdle my judgment is that Christians fare well. Their concept of God may be strange in the sense that outsiders wonder why they find it so convincing, but it is broadly clear to most people what they mean with their God-talk. An important test of clarity is whether we can see what the notion in question implies. Early in the next chapter when we look more fully into the Christian concept of God its implications will be spelt out at length, which naturally means that things are adequately clear. You can't do that with hopelessly confused ideas. However, it must in fairness be noted that there are some sceptical philosophers, such as Kai Nielsen, who find that they can make no sense of the concept of God, but they are the exceptions, not the rule.

The same holds for coherence. No factual implications follow from talk about square circles because the idea is nonsensical and cannot possibly refer to anything in the real world. But what is self-contradictory or incoherent about the notion of an almighty, everlasting and perfectly loving being? Squares cannot be round, but why could there not perhaps be a spiritual being who has the qualities Christians say belong to God, a being entirely free of the limitations and blemishes that we and all other things possess? I myself can see no reason for accusing Christians of incoherence in their basic idea of God, and neither do most sceptics, for example Bertrand Russell and Antony Flew, for why would they discuss evidence for and against the existence of God (as they have done) if they could show that the idea cancels itself? Nobody with any sense discusses evidence for married bachelors or round squares, because the very idea is hopelessly confused. Just to debate the evidence for the existence of God, as countless sceptics do, means that they find the concept coherent enough to indicate something that could possibly exist – unlike square circles.

The second requirement is that any factual claims being made in the debate must be supported by valid and appropriate evidence. If things are said about the world or about history, these must be confirmed by the first-hand investigation of competent judges. If God-talk means certain things about the past, then historians must verify them, and so too with scientific matters, each type of expert using the normal methods of that field of study. Not only is this requirement fair to the sceptics' demand for stringent testing. It is also fair to believers because they say they have found the objective truth about reality. This second requirement gives them an opportunity to prove their point. At the same time it accepts a class of evidence which is very important to them, namely the evidence of their own experience as believers. As we will see in later chapters, this appeal to experience plays a significant part in the debate about God.

Christian belief in God is of course much more than just a set of factual claims about history and the cosmos. It is a whole world-view, so there is a further aspect to the requirement of factual accuracy. This further aspect applies to any world-view, namely that it must fit our total knowledge of things (as produced by human experience generally and by the various branches of study) better than its rivals. I shall have more to say about this aspect of my method below in the section called 'Types of problem and levels of proof', and will apply it in chapter 4 when we judge the merits of the Christian world-view in the light of its critics' objections and counter-arguments.

The third criterion is that any arguments constructed by Christians and their critics must be logical. Sometimes conservative Protestants say that the things of God are higher than merely human logic, but even if this is so, the fact remains that their God-talk and everybody else's is still human God-talk. It may originate with God but once it comes to expression on our own lips in languages like English or French, it is obviously human. And at the human level, a rejection of logicality is the surest way for believers to damage their own case in the eyes of mentally and morally admirable people. Without logic we cannot have truth, because we could not tell the difference between true and false. Without it we cannot have goodness, because we could not distinguish between good and evil. Small wonder, then, that many thoughtful Christians welcome the chance to show what they see as the logical power of their arguments. They know that anything else is deeply harmful to their cause.

As well as these three truth-related norms I will also use an ethical criterion, where appropriate, in order to judge the practical value of a given belief. The norm in question is inclusive well-being. Since all the great religions accept it, as well as the most widespread secular ethical viewpoint in our culture (which sees the happiness of the greatest number as the best way to settle moral problems), this is an eminently fair norm to use. Who could quarrel with increasing the physical, moral and spiritual well-being of all? At issue in this book is not just the traditional Christian concept of God but also the values and lifestyles it encourages, so we would clearly be correct to evaluate the practical aspect of theism as well. In words I once heard by Peruvian philosopher Marisa de Poppe, 'It is not the tongue but our lives that must sing the new song.'

To summarize: the criteria that will come into play when weighing the arguments for and against belief in God are both theoretical and practical. We must ask of that belief not just how likely it is to be true, but also whether it elevates believers and societies into a better life. Christianity is a way of life associated with a set of beliefs about

13

God and Christ, so it invites us to judge its ethical quality as well as the quality of its doctrines. What could be fairer than that?

Grounds and processes of faith

With these points about fair criteria in mind and in view of the strangeness of widespread faith in a God whom nobody apparently ever directly detects, we must now ask the following question: why are so many people convinced of his existence? This question has both a factual and a philosophical answer. The factual answer is that the vast majority of these people believe in God because their faith was kindled by trusted, older people when they were very young, people like parents, priests and teachers. A smaller number found faith in God – through Jesus Christ, of course – because of conversion experiences later in life. Often this happens during the teens but is not limited to that time of life. Generally it is based on a strongly emotional and biblical appeal of the kind issued by the famous television evangelists in America. Very rarely indeed, a few people are led to belief in God by an intellectual search which ends with the conclusion that faith is a more rational position than its rivals.

In this book we shall not be mainly concerned with this factual matter of how so many people in our culture come to be convinced that there is indeed a God. Our concern is not how faith forms, but how sound it is. Grounds for theism rather than its social and personal functioning are what matter. Long ago sincere, devoted parents used to tell their children that the earth was flat, but the fact remains that they were wrong. Might that also be true of Christian belief in God? Only if we set aside the channelling of such belief and concentrate on its validity will we find the answer. In other words, the debate about God has more to do with philosophy of religion than sociology of religion, and that is why I said above that our question has both a factual side and a philosophical side, with the latter being our main concern. All the same, we cannot do justice to the centrality of Christ in Christian theism without some reference to the processes that kindle faith in God in his followers, as I shall show in the next chapter.

The God Question Today

Types of problem and levels of proof

Different problems have different methods and levels of proof. Suppose we hear it said that there is oil under New York City. This is a matter for geography and geology, and the way to settle it is to drill in the alleged area and see whether we strike oil. In this way the claim can sooner or later be settled conclusively. Suppose, next, that we move from geography to history and are told that the ancient Greeks got most of their best ideas from Egypt and Phoenicia. Here too we want to know whether the assertion is true or false. But the method of settling it changes because we cannot observe the past. So we must make do with indirect methods. There is also much more to assess than in the previous example, where a single item – oil – was at issue. Now a complex process of cultural borrowing in ancient times is at issue, making it much harder to settle the question.

In problems of this kind we cannot have the certainty that is possible with observable, present-day problems, so we settle them at a different level – the level of probability. We seek out all the evidence that can be found and weigh it carefully. If the scale balances, then the matter is inconclusive and we suspend judgment until fresh evidence tips the scale one way or the other. Otherwise we accept whatever conclusion seems more likely, while always remaining open to fresh evidence if it comes to light. And the more the scale tips to one side, the more firmly we are entitled to believe that the ancient Greeks either did or did not borrow their best ideas from their African and Asiatic neighbours.

Now we must consider a third example. Somebody says, 'Life has a purpose.' We remember Shakespeare, where we heard that history is a tale told by an idiot, full of sound and fury, signifying nothing, and we wonder whether life really does have a purpose. Here too the statement is regarded as true by the person who said it and false by others, so it is like our two previous examples in this respect. In the technical language of philosophy, all three statements – geographical, historical and metaphysical – have a truth-value, which means that they are capable of being either true or false, unlike commands or questions. But what about the way to settle this third type of statement? Unlike oil gushing from a well in Manhattan, 'purpose'

15

is not the sort of thing we can observe. It is a more mysterious, subtle sort of thing. Yet without a sense of purpose, many people find life as hard to endure as it is hard to move a car without petrol, so questions of purpose are also important to us in their own way. For some people they are vastly more important than anything else because they provide life with a sort of inner map and thus help us locate our own lives on it. In short, they give meaning to life for such people.

Another difference is thus that questions about a possible purpose in life affect us inwardly in a way that is quite unlike Manhattan oil or ancient Greek borrowings. Technically speaking we may call them *existential* problems because they affect our inner existence as persons. And whether we agree that life has a purpose or not will therefore depend on a combination of our personal experiences and our knowledge of life as a whole for all other people as well. It will need a careful, judicious, sensitive review of all those considerations in a spirit of great self-honesty, but even then we shall hardly reach the sort of public certainty that would be experienced about oil in New York City. What often happens is that people experience a personal or private certainty about their own world-view, but this on its own has little or no persuasive power for other people. To convince *them* there has to be a more objective demonstration that a given world-view is sounder than its rivals. No world-view has ever succeeded in winning the acceptance of a majority of thoughtful, informed people on this planet, which itself shows just how hard it is to move from personal to objective certainty in matters of this kind.

A cumulative argument

The point of these examples is to show that we cannot reasonably expect the statement 'there is an almighty and perfectly loving God' to be verified or falsified as clearly as simple matters of scientific fact or even quite complex historical issues. A better analogy is our third example because the God-question is also a profoundly self-involving or existential question. We could say that it involves the same complex process of seeking and weighing sets of arguments and evidence as our historical example, only much more so, as well as having the existential subtlety and blend of personal and public factors of our purpose-in-life example. Following an influential proposal by the British philosopher of religion Basil Mitchell in his book *The Justification of Theism*, this approach to the God-question has become known as a 'cumulative case' argument because it involves a process of adding together a whole set of arguments none of which wins the debate on its own but which amounts in the end to a balance of probability in favour of the believer. What else, in any case, would we expect when limited human enquirers tackle so vast and mysterious a question?

The next point to be clarified is related to what I have just said, namely that the very concept of God as taught by Christians leads logically to history and science as appropriate arenas of evidence. As I showed in a previous section, God-talk is also humanity-talk and world-talk because it says that this is a God-designed and God-willed universe and we are a God-designed and God-willed species. This surely means (if such a God in fact exists) that if we look deeply enough we will find that the world and human history point the open-minded truth-seeker towards the God whose infinite love pervades and anchors all things. And this is why the case for Christian theism involves more than personal, day-by-day experience of a God who appears utterly real to believers, and more also than the authority of Jesus Christ, central though that is for Christians, but also includes arguments drawn from philosophy, history, science, morality and religion, confirmed – so Christians say – by vivid religious experiences and by miracles.

My final point about method is that this book does not discuss the mediaeval attempts to prove that God exists, as attempted by famous church thinkers like Thomas Aquinas and Anselm of Canterbury. Nor does it discuss more recent arguments like William Paley's theory that the universe, being allegedly like a gigantic clock, cannot possibly just have happened on its own. Where there is a watch, he argued, there must be a watch-maker. Modern ideas have either made these older arguments obsolete, shown them to be sterile, or produced better versions of them. And in practice those who debate the existence of God in our day do not try to cover such old and seemingly infertile ground, for there are much more interesting and important ways of proceeding, as we will see. Keeping in mind these explanations about method, let us now turn to the main task of this book, which is to guide readers through the fascinating, often tricky but always hugely important modern debate about God.

2

The Case for the Believer

Few places on earth are more scenically majestic than Rio de Janeiro, and over that great city the towering statue of Christ the Redeemer raises its hands in blessing from the Corcovado hill. Similarly, the crucified carpenter of Nazareth dominates the skyline of Christian faith, convincing his followers world-wide that their belief in God is indeed sound. But they have additional arguments as well, so that the best case in support of their faith in God is a combination of arguments based on Christ and those other ones.

In this chapter I shall explain how the case works, starting with Christianity's unique understanding of God, so that we can know exactly what is at issue in the debate. The rest of the chapter then deals mainly with the individual arguments which Christians think further justify their belief in that God. These arguments are of two basic kinds: those which call our attention to various important facts accepted by all of us, which believers say point most logically to a God as their cause; and secondly an appeal to the personal experience of believers for whom God is convincingly real. We could think of these two kinds of argument as, on one hand, a collection of objective arguments about the world around us and about human existence, plus an appeal to personal experience which gives believers a deep sense of subjective or inner assurance about God on the other. The objective arguments are held to provide believers with sufficient grounds for considering that their inner, subjective assurance is no mere delusion or wishful thinking, but rests instead on very sound foundations in fact and in logic.

The set of objective arguments begins with what believers say are the historical facts about Jesus of Nazareth, together with related references to biblical history which they say lead up to and flow from him. Next, our attention is directed to the cosmos itself as grasped by philosophy, physics and biology. The facts of order and complexity are cited as especially important pieces of evidence pointing towards a God as their cause. Then the focus of interest narrows further to what we could call objective facts concerning human nature, morality and religion. Here too believers argue that the best explanation for these things is a God. Having dealt with them, Christians then add what they regard as confirmation of their position from two further facts, namely miracles and religious experiences, so rounding off the set of objective factors which they think conclusively supports their case. That done, they point to something we cannot publicly observe but which carries great personal conviction and is of course implicit in all religious experience, namely the believers' inner sense of what seems to be the direct presence of God in their lives, usually in the form of Christ or the Holy Spirit.

In what follows the case for the believer will follow this way of classifying the various arguments. Traditionally, however, believers have often used a different classification. They have argued that their faith finds justification from two quarters: firstly, revelations supposedly given by the God they believe in, taking the form of special interventions in history, and secondly the broad sweep of nature in its ordinary workings, where the unprejudiced mind can supposedly see the hand of a divine creator. For Christians this traditional view was classically expressed by St Paul himself in the first chapter of his letter to the Romans, where he wrote about Christ and the scriptures as coming from God, and then in verse 20 wrote that God's eternal power and divine nature can be perceived in the things he has made, namely nature.

The reason I have classified the believer's arguments differently is to avoid begging the question in favour of Christianity by accepting prematurely its notion of divine revelation. This idea requires a prior assurance that there is a God who reveals himself or his will, and that has not yet been established in the debate we are about to enter. The traditional Christian way of classifying the arguments in favour of their position can, however, be easily and fairly related to my way of setting them out, so there is no distortion involved. Let me explain the connection. According to Christians, divine revelation happens in Jesus himself, in the Bible (or at least key parts of it) and certain biblical events like the Exodus and Pentecost; in miracles and in individual religious experiences such as visions and dreams. Each of these appears in the set of arguments that follows, while the arguments based on the facts of nature and of human existence correspond to the traditional view that the world around us shows us the hand of a divine creator. In short, my classification includes everything cited by Christians but without any unfair bias in their favour.

The culmination of the believer's case is to gather all these individual arguments into a whole which we could call the Christian world-view, the point now being that the arguments must also be seen as a totality in order to appreciate their superiority over rival world-views. And with this outline of the case for theism in mind, we can turn now to a detailed discussion of each of the steps involved in it.

The Christian view of God

God as limitless love

When Christians in the historic mainstream of their faith talk about God they have in mind a single, invisible, personal spirit, all-powerful and perfectly good, the creator of all things, who hears the prayers of those who call on him, whose will is the greatest power in the universe, and – above all – who loves his creation with an everlasting and perfect love. He inspired the prophets of ancient Israel from Moses to John the Baptist; in his perfect love he entered history in bodily form as the unique saviour Jesus Christ, he works miracles according to his sovereign will, and his Holy Spirit, available to all believers, inspired the biblical writers, guides the church and leads Christians now and always.

There are other great concepts of God as a single, supreme being, like those of Judaism, Islam, Africa and parts of Hinduism. Scholars therefore often use the term monotheism for all such faiths, from the Greek words *monos* (= one) and *theos* (= god). These other monotheisms generally agree with Christianity about the perfect, limitless goodness and power of God and his lordship over the universe he created. But in giving a definition of the Christian view of God I am not concerned with the specific teachings of those other religions, only with Christianity because this book is about the soundness of Christian theism.

Therefore I must lay special emphasis on four distinctive brush-strokes made by Christians in their great painting of the deity. These concern Jesus of Nazareth and the idea of the Trinity. From Jesus the church has received and made central the belief that love is the main quality of God, so that we must attach special importance to this belief in what follows. Next, Christianity teaches that although God is a single being, yet in a mysterious way there is a threefold reality within the divine life which Christians speak of as God the Father, God the Son and God the Holy Spirit, each of them fully and equally divine. This is of course the famous doctrine of the Trinity. Thirdly, Christians regard the founder of their faith as no mere inspired human being but as God the Son, the second person in the Trinity, who became a flesh-and-blood person for the salvation of the world from sin and damnation, however these may be defined. Fourthly, there is the belief that God continues to be richly, lovingly and inspiringly available in the form of what Christians call the Holy Spirit, the third person in the Trinity.

Whole libraries have been written about this view of God. But I think it is true to say that the heart of all those millions of words is the conviction that the one true God is an infinitely and perfectly *loving* being. Almighty and just he certainly also is, say Christians, but his endless power is ultimately the power of limitless love and is never less than perfectly loving in the way it works. For this reason we must treat as secondary those other doctrines which admittedly also receive emphasis from many Christians, doctrines which portray God above all as the wielder of absolute power, issuing commands and requiring obedience on the part of his followers. No doubt there is biblical teaching to encourage this way of understanding the deity as directly causing or 'predestining' everything that happens, and even more in the writings of influential Christian leaders like St Augustine, John Calvin and others. But that is not the heart of the vision of God which Jesus of Nazareth passed on to his followers, so far as I can see, and we must not therefore allow it to lead us into an inaccurate view of the distinctively Christian understanding of the divine, namely that God is love and that in him there is nothing loveless whatsoever.

Implications of God's limitless love

In order to understand the Christian world-view more fully we must now take note of the wider implications of their belief that there truly exists a God whose power is limitlessly and unfailingly loving. When we do so we find something that is undeniably impressive.

The first of these implications is what Christians call the grace of God, meaning his gift of himself. As the loving source and basis of reality, God's nature expresses itself, say Christians, in a boundless giving of life, bringing the multitude of created things into being so that that they can receive his love and return it and relate to one another in a loving way. Love cannot exist in solitude. It must express itself in the giving and receiving of love – as David Jenkins said, God is either gift or delusion. Therefore creativity is one of the hallmarks of genuine love, meaning the act of bringing into being new occasions of love. And an infinite love does so in an endlessly rich way. To put the matter slightly differently, a God of perfect love cannot have planned a universe that would function, at heart, in a way that contradicts his own nature. And since the universe gets its own essential nature wholly from God, who alone is almighty, it cannot ultimately thwart his fundamental intentions as creator. Accordingly, everything is as it is and operates as it does because of God's loving charter for the entire cosmos, either through his direct, second-by-second control as some Christians think, or because he gives it a range of possibilities, a sufficiency of energy and a degree of real freedom to unfold on its own within the ultimate framework of his loving intention.

Thus the first aspect of the infinite love of God is his gift of his own nature in the creative act of making the universe. Christians therefore say that the universe (meaning everything other than God) arises from nothing but his loving power and plan. This, of course, is the famous doctrine of creation *ex nihilo* – the creation of the universe from nothing.

But the grace of God is not spent by the act of originating the universe. Being perfect and without limit, God ceaselessly pours forth the abundance of his love, an unfailing cascade of life-giving water in the dry lands of the cosmos. Christians receive from Judaism the belief that this can be seen in the history of ancient Israel, interpreting the story of Abraham, the liberation of the Hebrew slaves from Egypt under Moses, their conquest of the land of Canaan under Joshua and the words of the Hebrew prophets as instances of God's continuing care.

But above all they see it confirmed and perfected in Jesus of Nazareth, declaring his entire existence to be the ultimate demonstration of God's unfailing love, continuing beyond his bodily presence as the power of the Holy Spirit bringing renewed life and love to believers. In the words of William Plomer's poem 'A Church in Bavaria', they see here 'a sunrise of love enlarged'. And as a logical extension of these ideas, they believe that in the end the future will see the final triumph of God's love. Death cannot have the last word in a drama of endless love. Beyond the grave, therefore, awaits life made whole by God's love for all who open their lives to him. As Luther once remarked, that which God touches is certainly made immortal. How could it be otherwise if God is eternally and almightily loving?

The next implication of this view of God is that there is no getting away from his presence. If the kind of God believed in by Christians really exists then it follows that everything else that exists – absolutely everything – always does so in the invisible presence of this infinite love. The writing or reading of these words, the rain and the winds, the births and deaths of all things, every human venture or effort including all debates about God and quite literally everything else that has ever happened or ever will, they all happen within the endless depths and range of that divine love. Obviously God does not desire sin or evil, but that does not mean that people who commit evil somehow enter an area where God's loving presence is excluded. Moreover, the divine love which Christians say enfolds us is rich and complete, in contrast with the uneven and often faltering love which is the best we humans can manage. Similarly, it is unfailingly constant; it never wavers or lapses into anything harsh, mean-spirited or unloving, even when it encounters things like cruelty and oppression which run counter to it. Obviously a perfectly loving God cannot approve of such things or will them to happen. But that does not mean that he lapses into hatred and rejection when relating to people who act cruelly or hatefully.

Another implication of Christianity's concept of God is that our lives, along with absolutely everything else in creation, are irreplaceably precious to God, being the objects of his love. Our individual natures which make us unique are also therefore infinitely dear to him. We humans might find some things repulsive, but not so God; all things whatsoever are the receivers of his inexhaustible and all-powerful love, including those who reject him or give their lives over to evil. And because he is perfect, his love knows no favourites. All alike are infinitely and everlastingly dear to him. Therefore whoever hurts or destroys anything in the universe, harms that which God, with all the endless resources of his being, cherishes without reservation, and is thus in outright conflict with him, the greatest power of all.

But in no way could God ever relate to those who inflict such harm or destruction in anything but a supremely loving manner. Love's way is to promote – selflessly if need be – the well-being of those it loves, to long for their safety, fulfilment and happiness, and do all that is possible to enable them to achieve those things. Infinite, perfect love must therefore do these things in an infinite, perfect and everlasting way, overflowing with love and concern for even the littlest of things, the ants, the very grains of sand, the most fleeting of sub-atomic particles, and even for the vilest of things, morally speaking. All alike, great or small, saintly or wicked, belong ultimately to him and their greatest well-being is his eternal will for them. Their love for him in return and their flourishing in a framework of love must thus be his supreme desire, and their rejection or hatred must be his supreme challenge to overcome by means of love alone and the things it can do.

I know, of course, that many Christians, particularly conservatives, believe in Hell as a place or state where the unsaved suffer eternal separation from God. But the Christian concept of God's perfect love does not logically require that notion and may even preclude it, as we will see near the end of chapter 3, so it would be unfair to insist on building it into our account of God's nature. In any case, even if some people choose to exclude God from their lives (assuming for the moment that there is a God), that does not mean that *he* excludes them from his love.

In consequence, Christian faith in God cannot but also be a view of the entire universe as infinitely God-loved and precious, precious in as fundamental a way as anything could be for such believers. Thus a theology with perfect love as its hallmark translates into a cosmology and an anthropology – a world-view and a view of humanity – with love as their hallmark as well, and there can be no denying the inspiring power and beauty of such a faith with its vision of all things arising from and existing within the invisible, eternal presence of the God in whom Christians believe. It is thus entirely logical for Christians, believing that this basic reality is bodily present in Jesus of Nazareth, to think of their message as the greatest good news for the world.

Beautiful this belief certainly is, but it is also strange, precisely because the divine presence which believers say is so utterly real is also utterly invisible. We can see the fresh, bright sunlight of a new day illuminating our world. We can smell and feel the air around us. But nobody ever sees or in any other ordinary way detects the allegedly pervasive reality of God. And if he cares so utterly and all-powerfully for the well-being of all things, as Christians say, why is there so much destruction and misery? Why do the innocent suffer and the cruel prevail? Why are there such loveless scourges as Aids and cancer?

Why, in short, are Christians so sure that there really is such a God at all? Let us find out by turning now to the set of objective, factually-based arguments which believers say point to a God as their most probable cause, starting with the argument that Jesus Christ himself is centrally important in showing that God exists.

The Case for the Believer

The objective evidence: 1. The facts about Christ

Jesus as God incarnate

According to the four Gospels – our main source for the ideas and deeds of Jesus of Nazareth – the founder of Christianity taught that God is an infinitely loving, father-like being who summons all people into a life of active love for their fellows. Moreover, Jesus himself is shown as practising that kind of life so completely that he sacrificed his life for it to save us from our sins and their terrible consequence of separating us from God. But, says Christianity, the power of God intervened and Jesus rose from death so that the full truth about him, as John's Gospel says and as mainline Christianity asserts, is that he himself perfectly embodies God's presence in physical form as the incarnation of God the Son, second person of the Trinity, who entered history as the world's only saviour. His divine power accounts, furthermore, for the ability Christians see in him to do the miracles which are such a notable feature of the Gospels.

What he taught and did were taken up into the lives of his disciples, so creating a new religious movement. They in turn drew others into the faith in an ever-widening circle of devotion and obedience to the Jesus they hailed as Christ and Lord, like the latest annual ring on a tree, living a new kind of life centred upon him and upon the eternally loving God he both preached and was believed personally to embody. Today's Christians are thus the latest of those growth rings on the two-thousand-year-old tree of the church going back in continuity to Jesus himself.

For Christians, therefore, the justification for their concept of God is above all the living, historical reality of Jesus himself in word and deed, and he is authoritative because he speaks, according to Christians, with the voice of the infallible God himself. In the technical language of theology, the case for the Christian believer thus bases itself first and foremost, as I explained earlier in this chapter, on what believers see as divine revelation – meaning that God himself has allegedly shown that he exists and what he is like in the life of Christ.

Assuming for the moment that this view of things is true, then logically it means that anybody brought up in such a faith is raised within the circle of God's most direct impact and grows up knowing at first hand the unsurpassable blessings of a life lived in his loving power and grace. But what about thoughtful outsiders who enquire into these things? To them Christians say that while the proof lies ultimately in accepting Christ and experiencing for oneself the reality, grace and goodness of God in and through his only Son, a first step is to understand that there are conclusive, rational grounds for accepting what Jesus said about God because there are conclusive, rational grounds for accepting that Jesus is himself God in human form.

I know that there are Christians who differ at this point and say that one must simply believe in Christ, but that seems scarcely credible in a culture where blind belief is almost always a serious failing in every other important facet of life. We rightly think poorly of people who fatuously believe the talk they hear from used-car salesmen or who leap blindly into marriage, because they are being highly irresponsible. So how could it be otherwise with faith? A tyrannical God might demand unthinking acceptance but hardly a morally perfect one who supposedly gave us our minds in the first place, so the valid move by Christians cannot be an insistence on blind faith but rather the assertion that it is more rational to accept Jesus' message than to reject it.

What grounds are there for such an assertion? Christians themselves often take Christ's authority for granted, but are they correct? In the wider arena of the modern debate about God nothing can be taken for granted, and the truth about Jesus is thus something that must be established on factual and logical grounds, not just announced.

In responding to this reality, the Christian argument now takes a highly significant turn by becoming in effect an argument about the reliability of the New Testament picture of Jesus. He himself is not available for us to hear and question. What we have instead is an oral and a scriptural tradition about him. In considering them, I will however concentrate on the written tradition even though it is somewhat the later of the two and arose out of the earlier, word-of-mouth traditions of the fledgling church. I do so because the two are now so inextricably linked that they cannot in practice be separated

and because the oral tradition has for many centuries been
by the New Testament documents, which are of course t
core of the written Jesus tradition.

Let us remind ourselves briefly that the argument at this point runs
as follows: Christian belief in God is sound because it is first and
foremost anchored in the authority of God himself, made known to
humanity in bodily form in Jesus Christ, whose words and deeds
show us that God is real and that he has the loving, almighty nature
which Christianity says he has. And we are rationally justified in
accepting this – so the argument goes – because historically authentic
documents exist which prove beyond reasonable doubt that Jesus
existed, taught and acted just as the church says he did. Christians
therefore say that it is more logical to trust this New Testament
material about Jesus than to doubt it, at least in its essentials. Let us
look at this argument in more detail.

The reliability of the Gospels

There are four contentions in or arising from the Gospels (supported
by Paul's letters) which are vital to the Christian case for faith in
God. First of all – obviously – Jesus of Nazareth must really have
existed; secondly, he must in fact have taught that God is an infinitely
loving heavenly Father; thirdly, it must be shown that this view of
God is correct because Jesus was uniquely qualified to give it to the
world, being himself divine; and fourthly, it must be true that Jesus
had the power to perform miracles and – above all – that he rose
from the dead as a unique proof of the divine status Christians believe
him to have. As we shall see, this fourth point is especially important
for any rational argument in favour of Christian theism.

Fundamentalists often think that Christianity stands or falls on
the reliability of every line in the Bible but that is an unnecessarily
ambitious (and to my mind unattainable) proposal. All that is in fact
necessary is to validate the core of the Christian position, which I
have summarized in the four points above. It may be that there are
also independent ways of establishing that a God of perfect love
indeed exists, as theists claim, but for Christians there can be no
avoiding this appeal to the cardinal facts (if such they be) about
Jesus and thus also to the historical reliability of the relevant New

Testament writings which are the basic written source for all that we know about him.

Why, then, should an open-minded, truth-seeking person decide that those writings are trustworthy? To answer this question we have to turn to the principles governing the evaluation of documents on the part of qualified historians. From this quarter we learn that a document's credibility as a source depends on six factors. Firstly, the closer the document is to the persons or events it speaks of the better. Best of all are eyewitness records. This is why diaries, letters and other first-person reports are of particularly great importance to historians. And if the authors of such documents say things that actually run counter to their known interests, then those reports would in general have a very high level of trust-worthiness.

A second factor is the competence of the people who provide the reports in question. We naturally find the evidence of a balanced, educated adult with a reputation for honesty more plausible than we would the words of a drunken scoundrel or a partisan bigot, so it is always necessary to enquire about the kind of person who wrote whatever report we as historians may be evaluating. The third factor is independent confirmation, for we are naturally more likely to believe what two or more witnesses, who have not agreed to support each other, say happened than to accept an unconfirmed report. Fourthly, the contents of the documents before us should square with our existing knowledge of the situation they deal with. For example, we would reject an alleged report of a World War II battle in France during 1940 which mentioned American combat units or commanding officers, because America only entered the war in Europe at a later date.

Next, the evidence must in general have an inherent plausibility if it is to be taken seriously as historical fact. Texts which tell of talking horses or water flowing uphill obviously strike us as extremely suspect. Lastly, the evidence being judged must pass whatever technical tests might apply. For example, the alleged Hitler diaries several years ago were analysed by hand-writing experts and found to be suspect, and it was finally proved that the Shroud of Turin could not be the burial cloth of Christ when scientific dating tests showed beyond doubt that the cloth itself originated in the Middle Ages.

The case for trusting the Gospel picture of Jesus enlists each of these principles in its favour. While it is true, of course, that none of the New Testament comes to us from the pen of Jesus himself, the important parts of it are impressively close to the events they describe, considering how long ago those events were. St Paul's letters, which include the oldest New Testament texts, were written over a period lasting from about a decade until at most about thirty years after the life of Christ. The four Gospels are not themselves, say the majority of experts, the work of eye-witnesses but almost certainly used such witnesses as sources, or at least rest ultimately on them. They were written from roughly thirty years (Mark's Gospel) to about sixty years after the events they discuss in the case of John's Gospel (though this is disputed by some), and were thus produced while eye-witnesses were still alive to refute errors, at least in the case of Mark's Gospel. While we have no proof that this actually happened, at least part of the Gospel material is old enough to have been subject to the corrective influence of living eye-witnesses or others who knew their testimony at first hand.

Admittedly this means that the New Testament – when judged by the norms of ordinary, historical standards – cannot be placed in the highest category of reliability so far as closeness to the relevant events is concerned because none of it in present form comes from the pen of Christ himself or is the work of eye-witnesses of events in his life. But nonetheless it fares well enough on this score to merit being taken very seriously indeed. By the standards of ancient history the New Testament events are in fact richly documented – better than the careers of the Roman emperors of that time, for example, and vastly better than the career of Moses or any other figure before the time of King David in the history of ancient Israel.

What about the competence of the New Testament writers? It must obviously be granted that they were all devotees of Jesus and were thus naturally favourable towards him. This is especially true of Paul. He had been a zealous, persecuting opponent of the fledging church in Palestine before that most famous of all conversion experiences turned him into the exact opposite, a passionate and tireless supporter. It is only fair to concede that people with that kind of history sometimes show a notable bias in favour of their new loyalty and an equally strong aversion to their former one. Christians often say that divine guidance means that Paul's personal failings (if such they be) can be set aside as irrelevant, but at this stage of the debate – when the existence of God has yet to be established – that is merely to beg the question and is an invalid move. This means that we must be alert to the possibility of a significant element of partiality on his part, understandable though that would be.

There is thus no denying the presence of a significant interest on the part of the New Testament writers (and not just Paul) in furthering the aims of their new religion. But there are also important factors which count strongly in their favour. The very fact that those authors could write Greek means that they were among the educated elite in a generally illiterate culture. Some of them, notably Paul and Luke, were in fact highly educated, the equivalent in today's world of university-educated people. And it is surely fair to accept them as morally sound because of the sheer unlikelihood that cheats and liars would join the Jesus-movement at a time when the movement was experiencing a good deal of official harrassment and persecution. When weighed against these strongly favourable facts, the admitted bias of the New Testament writers in favour of Jesus cannot be regarded as seriously affecting their general credibility, let alone destroying it.

Turning now to the third criterion of good evidence, it is fortunate for Christians that the early church included no less than four Gospels when they finalized the contents of the New Testament, because this means that we do not have to rely on a single, unsupported piece of evidence. Careful study of those Gospels has however shown that we cannot treat them as fully independent sources. Most of Mark's Gospel is repeated in Matthew and Luke in a way which means that they had it before them when writing their Gospels, adding material from a second source which they also both used, known simply as 'Q' to biblical scholars (from the German word *Quelle*, meaning a source). In addition they both had their own unique sources for the material that is found exclusively in one or the other of those two Gospels. What we therefore have as the earliest written sources is, in all probability, the following: Mark, Q, Matthew's special source and Luke's special source. These certainly seem to be independent of one another – but against that must be weighed the fact that they contain different stories, not the same ones, so that they do not corroborate one another except in general terms.

Things are further complicated by John's Gospel because it has some important differences from the others. Let me mention just three of these differences. Jesus' ministry is shown as lasting several years, against the much shorter period implied by the other three gospels (known to scholars as the 'Synoptic Gospels'); he visits Jerusalem for the first time near the start of his ministry, not at the end; and he is portrayed as teaching typically in the form of long discourses rather than the shorter sayings so prevalent in the Synoptic Gospels. That there is a difficulty here cannot be denied, but it does not make the Gospels useless as historical sources, and I do not think it is a serious historical problem for anybody other than fundamentalists and conservative Christians who think that a line-by-line biblical accuracy is essential. For the project of this book it is not really significant at all, because all we need is assurance about the four central points about Jesus that were listed above – that he existed, that he said God was a perfectly loving, father-like being, that he as God the Son uniquely embodies God in human form and therefore speaks with the authority of God himself, and that he had miraculous powers and rose from the dead as proof of his divine nature.

So far as these four points are concerned, the question is whether we have corroborated evidence or not, and here the picture is much more rosy than for biblical fundamentalism and conservative evangelicalism. That Jesus of Nazareth genuinely existed and preached a new religious message in the context of his native Judaism at that time is almost universally accepted by friend and foe, so that it is only in the rarest of cases that we find anybody with scholarly standing trying to argue a contrary view – for example the British scholar G.A. Wells. We even have a few small but valuable pieces of independent Jewish and Roman historical evidence that Jesus of Nazareth was a real, historical person and not a mythical being. That his message was centred upon the idea of God's coming kingdom as a reality characterized above all by the outpouring of his fatherly love is shown by all the Gospel sources, admittedly not in every detail (for example, only Luke contains the parable of the Good Samaritan), but certainly as the overall theme of his message.

Similar consensus exists concerning Jesus' teachings about his own special intimacy with God the Father, though admittedly Jesus himself is nowhere explicitly reported as saying that he was God incarnate or that God is a Trinity. Likewise, all the Gospel sources agree that he had wonder-working powers, though the agreement is stronger in connection with miracles of healing than for the so-called nature miracles like walking on the water and stilling storms on the Sea of Galilee.

The fourth requirement by historians when testing their sources is whether they fit into our existing facts about the topic in question. Here too the New Testament fares well enough to earn respect as a source. The story told in it claims to have happened at a definite point in Roman and Jewish history, because the names of the leaders of those two peoples are given. Pontius Pilate, before whom Jesus was tried, is the best known example. Place names are given, for example the cities and towns of Galilee and Judaea. From other historical and geographical sources we know that the Gospel picture fits very well into our existing knowledge. But the fit is a general one, adding plausibility to the Gospel record in a general rather than a specific way. There simply are no other sources for the details of that record, for example Jesus choosing his disciples or what he said at the start of his ministry in the synagogue at Nazareth, as reported by Luke. So although sceptics cannot say that the New Testament clashes with our knowledge from other sources, neither can Christians claim that there is a detailed correspondence either, though they can claim a broad consistency with our independent knowledge of the situation. And that in itself is important.

So far as the fifth criterion – inherent plausibility – is concerned, we have a mixed situation caused by the miraculous element in the New Testament. Most secular-minded people (and many believers) find stories about Jesus walking on the water or feeding five thousand people with a few loaves and fishes – not to speak of rising from the dead – utterly far-fetched and implausible, because such things are totally out of line with ordinary human experience. How many of us, for example, could certify in public that we have observed such things ourselves in circumstances with little or no chance of deception or delusion? But for the rest, the Gospel picture of Jesus raises few problems of this kind. Of the four key facts about Jesus that were listed at the start of this section, the first two (that Jesus existed and that he taught about God as an ever-loving heavenly father) contain nothing that is inherently implausible. The third fact concerns the Gospel claim that Jesus said he himself had a special closeness to the Father, especially those passages in the Gospels where Jesus reportedly identified himself with God. For example, John's Gospel reports him as saying that 'I and the Father are one.' That would be blasphemy for a Jew, so some readers see this as very implausible. But this latter type of utterly startling statement lacks adequate confirmation elsewhere in the Gospels, so we should be careful about insisting that it is historically authentic. What is not in doubt is Jesus' sense of special closeness with what he took to be his heavenly Father, and while that may seem a pretentious or mistaken claim to non-Christians, they can hardly say that it is inherently implausible.

This leaves us with the fourth part of the Jesus tradition, namely the miracles, which is where problems of implausibility arise. But implausibility is not the same as impossibility. Whether Jesus in fact had miraculous powers, and above all whether he rose from the dead, depends mainly on the quality of the evidence, not on what common sense tells us is unlikely. Common sense can be wrong, but strong evidence commands the respect of open-minded people. So we must now ask how strong the evidence is for the miraculous element in the Gospel tradition. The really important miracle story is of course the resurrection, so that is what we need to examine.

But first we must consider the remaining historical test, namely that the evidence being studied should pass relevant technical tests like carbon-dating a fragment from the Shroud of Turin. This requirement also presents no problems for Christians. The oldest manuscripts of the New Testament are written, for instance, on materials and in a style that arouse no suspicion of forgery. On the other hand, none of them is an original either, for the original texts have all perished (the so-called 'lost autographs') leaving us only with copies of copies. But these have not been found defective on technical grounds, so we need not spend any more time discussing this final way of checking whether the Gospel sources really are genuine.

Taken together, then, these standard tests fail to uncover anything suspicious about the Gospel sources other than the seeming implausibility of the miraculous element, which will be discussed in the next section. Certainly there are no good grounds, so far as I am concerned, for disputing that there really was a person nearly two thousand years ago in Palestine whom we call Jesus of Nazareth, that he taught a message emphasizing the tender, fatherly love and care of a God for whom all things were possible, and that he claimed to have a special intimacy with God, perhaps even that of God's unique son. This leaves us with the stories about his alleged miraculous rising from the dead and the miracles he is said to have performed. What about these?

The resurrection as fact

How sound is the resurrection tradition? Is there enough evidence to overcome our natural sense that such things just don't happen? As I pointed out earlier, when a source mentions implausible things like talking horses we are entitled to be highly sceptical because they run counter to the uniform experience of the entire human race so far. It would take truly outstanding evidence and plenty of it to outweigh such scepticism. A dead person rising from the tomb, never to die again, may not be as utterly implausible as a talking horse or a flying elephant to people who are used to the idea, but it does go against our unvarying experience, so the evidence will have to be very strong indeed to overcome the natural scepticism it arouses.

Let us notice here that the truth of the resurrection stories is very important for orthodox, traditional Christianity's form of belief in God. It cannot be seriously doubted that Jesus of Nazareth spoke of a God who is perfectly and everlastingly loving. Having seen some good evidence of faith-healers myself, I also have no difficulty accepting that Jesus had remarkable, perhaps unequalled, healing powers. But neither those healing powers nor his vision of God by themselves amount to anything more than the work of a human religious genius. That God loves with a fatherly love is not itself an original idea of Jesus', for it occurred in the Jewish tradition long before him, for example the Book of Hosea. And healing skills can quite plausibly be regarded as having their basis in psychological and physical processes of a purely natural kind which we have not yet discovered, just as nuclear power or hypnotism were once undiscovered. If Jesus' concept of God is correct and not just an attractive fiction then we need more than just his words and healings.

Many well-informed, thinking Christians concede that we do not have sufficiently good evidence to establish as at least highly probable that Jesus performed miracles of nature. The accounts of these supposed nature miracles in the Gospels are very brief, undetailed, uncorroborated and patchy in comparison with the accounts of the resurrection. There is no way in which they can convince fair-minded but critical enquirers that Jesus must be divine. Everything therefore depends on the resurrection having really happened, and only a truly powerful collection of evidence will convince the open-minded, fair enquirer that it did. Christians who take the resurrection for granted need to make the effort to understand how things *validly* look to outsiders on this score, and accept that they are entitled to evidence of a very high quality indeed.

Let us see, then, how good the evidence is that Jesus rose from death never to die again, starting with the documentary evidence. This comes in the form of six New Testament passages comprising the resurrection accounts given at the end of all four Gospels, a brief reference to it by Peter mentioned in Acts 2.24, and a longer reference by Paul in I Corinthians 15.3-8. In their present form these passages date from about twenty years after the event in Paul's case to as much as sixty years. Interested readers should study them carefully, and they will then see for themselves that their character as evidence can be summarized as follows. They all assert or strongly imply that Jesus rose from the dead, though no claim is made that anybody actually witnessed the resurrection itself, but they also contain many discrepancies about the exact details of this alleged happening. In particular, they disagree about the fairly important question of who saw the risen Jesus first, for while the Gospels agree that it was Mary of Magdala, probably accompanied by one or two other women (note the further discrepancies here), our oldest source, Paul, says that Jesus first appeared to Cephas, the Aramaic form of the name Peter.

None of these six passages is itself a personal, eye-witness account of the events that supposedly took place that first Easter Sunday in and near the tomb of Jesus. However, the Gospels clearly imply that Peter was one of those to whom the risen Christ appeared and that he had earlier seen the empty tomb. Though there is no mention of this in the brief account Luke gives in Acts 2.24 (in the form of Peter's own words, which makes it somewhat surprising that Peter mentioned nothing of his own personal contact with the risen Jesus in a context where such a reference would have greatly strengthened his own argument), we know that Paul had met Peter, so Paul's passage about the resurrection has a strong claim to rest directly on the evidence of at least one eye-witness. But on the other hand, the more we emphasize the value of Paul's evidence, the more this raises problems for the credibility of the Gospel material, at least so far as details are concerned, because Paul gives a markedly different account of the names and sequence of the alleged eye-witnesses from those given in the four Gospels – and they have their own, lesser, mutual discrepancies. Furthermore, Paul's evidence – the oldest and closest (so far as we can tell) to an alleged eye-witness – is entirely about Jesus appearing to a series of people from Cephas (i.e. Peter) to Paul himself. It contains nothing at all about an empty tomb or any details of those supposed appearances.

Clearly, belief in the bodily resurrection of Jesus, and hence also in the deity who is said to have raised him, cannot be evoked solely by these biblical accounts. They lack the corroborated, eye-witness consistency and detail that would be needed to induce acceptance by a fair and open-minded judge as establishing the probability that Jesus rose bodily from the dead, let alone the certainty that he rose. Nonetheless, this documentary evidence from the New Testament cannot on that account be dismissed as a fabrication either. It agrees in broad terms that such a resurrection indeed happened, some of it (at least) comes from the pens of highly educated, responsible authors, and all of it comes from authors whose moral integrity we have every reason to respect. There is also sufficiently close access to at least one

supposed eye-witness to make it highly unreaso[...]
evidence as clearly unsound.

We are therefore left by the written evidence, tak[...]
a position midway between acceptance and rejecti[...]
aspects of the evidence incline a fair and open-minde[...] wards
accepting that Jesus probably did rise from the dead, however
awkward that may seem to our secular culture, but the negative
aspects, seen in relation to the sheer unlikelihood of such an event
really happening, induce an equivalent scepticism. In short, the
written evidence leaves the case wide open. But that, say Christians,
is itself a major achievement, given the extent and depth of the doubts
that must naturally exist about so utterly unprecedented a claim.

History supports the resurrection

So much for the documentary evidence. But it would be very unfair
to leave matters there because there is another category of evidence
to be considered. This is the clear fact that very soon after the
shocking, public death of Jesus, his followers rallied into a movement
convinced that he had in fact risen from the dead, openly declaring
this conviction in the face of the very authorities in Jerusalem who
had put him to death in the first place. Obviously they were not
converted to this conviction by the New Testament writings, which
did not exist at that time. What convinced them, say Christians, was
an experience or set of experiences of Jesus which made them sure
that he and his message had triumphed over death.

Let us be quite clear about certain things here. We may doubt
whether a bodily resurrection took place, but we cannot reasonably
doubt that at least some of Jesus' disciples were convinced of it –
convinced that he had appeared to them after the shocking events of
his crucifixion, and convinced also that his tomb was empty by
daybreak on that first Easter morning. The documentary evidence
for these convictions is exceptionally good. Nor can we reasonably
doubt that these disciples began to preach this message of a risen
Jesus within weeks of his death in Jerusalem itself – a very short
distance from the tomb and under the noses of those who had put
him to death. What could possibly have made the disciples act like
this other than the conviction that Jesus had indeed risen, knowingly

courting the reprisals of a set of authorities, both Jewish and Roman, who according to the Gospels had opposed their leader strongly enough to put him to death?

There can be no serious case for them preaching a lie. But it is certainly possible that they were sincerely deluded in believing that a bodily resurrection had taken place. Perhaps the authorities had removed Jesus' body secretly during that night after the Passover to prevent his grave becoming a rallying place for devotees. Perhaps word of the tomb from the women who then discovered it empty fused with powerful visions of Jesus and a dawning sense that his message was itself deathlessly valid, producing the natural, unconscious belief that a bodily resurrection had occurred. Thoughtful Christians concede that this is possible, but then counter by pointing out that such a theory makes it the easiest thing in the world for the authorities to have killed the new Christian movement by revealing that they had removed his body. Yet nothing of the kind is reported in either the Christian or the Jewish and Roman histories of the period. Instead, the opponents of the new religion alleged that the disciples themselves had stolen the body, but we have already seen that any theory which requires a conscious act of deceit by the disciples is the least likely one of all.

Thus Christians conclude not only that the first disciples came to believe unshakeably that Jesus had risen, risking and in some cases meeting death for their faith, but that the most rational explanation – by a process of eliminating the alternative possibilities – is that Jesus had in fact risen in the literal, bodily sense of that word. And they formed this conviction, so the relevant documents indicate, on the basis of personally experiencing his post-resurrection appearances, not by reading the documentary evidence we have so far been weighing in this chapter. The documentary evidence as we have it was written down several decades later, after the process of personally receiving and transmitting the Easter faith was firmly under way on the part of courageous founding members whose own lives had been made vehicles of the same love taught by Jesus.

The clear implication for the rational, open-minded enquirer is thus that a Jesus-centred theism arose – just when we would expect it to have fizzled out following the capture and execution of its only significant leader – because of the public fusion of three of the most powerfully persuasive factors available to humanity : first-hand experience in conditions ideally suited to the unmasking of pretence and delusion; the highest level of moral integrity (the kind found in people who prefer death to renouncing their beliefs); and a day-by-day transformation by the power of love. Within a few decades the movement launched in this way would produce a set of written evidences of its founding events, but the main instrument of its spread until the present has been that living continuity of faith transmitted from person to person, not the New Testament documents, least of all standing on their own as items in an archive. In due course children would be taught to believe unquestioningly in Jesus and his God from earliest childhood by devout Christian parents, but to start with in the ancient world of the Mediterranean and in all new areas it was adults who first had to be convinced. As the record shows, they *were* convinced. Christians therefore feel entitled to claim that the best available rational and factual explanation for the rise of the Christian movement is that its founder indeed rose from the dead. Nothing else, they say, will satisfactorily account for the success of the Jesus-movement.

And if we add this piece of historical evidence to the documentary evidence, then – say Christians – the balance of probability swings clearly in favour of the genuineness of the resurrection. I pointed out earlier in this chapter that Jesus' concept of God and his healing powers cannot suffice on their own to validate Christian theism. Something manifestly beyond the scope of any ordinary human power is needed to do that. The resurrection, say Christians, provides that validation; as something that is clearly beyond our human power to achieve, the resurrection must be God's doing and therefore it gives Jesus' message an authority beyond that of any ordinary human being. And once that is granted, then it is at once possible to grant, so the argument continues, that the stories about Jesus performing nature miracles like walking on the water are by no means incredible, for the superhuman power of God has been admitted as the best explanation for them.

But is this reasoning correct? Why should we simply accept that any event which is beyond our human ability to produce must have

God as its cause? Couldn't there be other possible causes? People who have been raised in a God-believing culture often miss the problem that others immediately spot at this point when God is cited as the only rational explanation for the resurrection. To experience its force, let us imagine somebody who comes from a culture which has never had a God-concept. On hearing Christians saying, 'Since no human could have raised Jesus, God must have done so', that person would immediately *and validly* interrupt and ask who or what God is – and why Christians think there is such a being in the first place. Otherwise, invoking a God at this point as presumed cause of the resurrection is merely an *ad hoc* hypothesis, and this is usually a weak move to make. Recognizing this, thoughtful Christians concede that the argument from the authority of Jesus, with its strong reliance on the contested conviction that he rose from the dead, cannot on its own give us an adequate argument for the existence of God. They recognize that extra grounds must now be given for their theism. These, say Christians, are in fact available in the form of certain highly significant sets of facts about the universe itself and about life on our own planet, especially human life, thereby bringing philosophy, physics, biology and philosophical anthropology into the debate. To these we therefore now proceed.

The objective evidence: 2. The nature of the cosmos

Philosophy and ultimate explanation

It has been said that the most basic question anybody could ask is the philosophical question why anything exists at all – why there is reality rather than sheer nothingness. There is a longstanding argument to the effect that the cosmos as a whole does not and cannot explain itself. By contrast, so that argument goes, only God could count as a satisfactory ultimate explanation for the fact that anything exists at all, because the word 'God' means an uncaused, eternal and perfect being. Another philosophical argument is that if anything is to exist at all, then a God is more likely than the universe because a single being like a God has greater prior probability than something as complex as the physical universe. And then there is also the mediaeval Muslim argument called the kalam cosmological argument, to the effect that the universe cannot be eternal. Christians are entitled to use this argument because it is logically appropriate to their faith as well as to Islam. We will look at these three philosophical arguments in turn.

An ultimate explanation can be defined as one which logically needs no further explanation. For example, I may ask why the Golden Gate Bridge exists, and be told that it was built to assist people north of San Francisco to travel to that city. Then I may ask why those people wanted to travel to San Francisco and be told that they needed work. That in turn makes me wonder why they needed work, and so on, each explanation giving rise to a new puzzle. This process either goes back infinitely (which means there is no ultimate explanation at which the process logically ends), or it culminates in a final step which introduces into the process a factor which is self-sufficient and therefore does not give rise to any further questions.

Believers argue that God, understood as an infinite, perfect, absolute and necessary being, would be precisely such a final reality, beyond whom it is not possible or necessary to go. Being perfect, God would need nothing and thus be fully self-sufficient, so it is illogical to ask what produced God. That kind of question only makes sense in relation to things that exist contingently, as philosophers say – things that could be different or could conceivably not have existed at all, and which need something else to bring them into being and make them what they are, like computers or chairs and people. To ask what caused a self-sufficient being is thus nonsensical; it is the same as asking what caused an uncaused being.

So if there is a God, he would logically qualify as the ultimate explanation for the universe, whereas everything else in the universe seems to depend on something else for its existence and cannot thus provide us with a really satisfactory answer to our original and most basic question – why anything exists at all. A *complete* account of reality would of course be possible only if we could identify something self-sufficient and powerful enough to give rise to everything else that exists and not itself need explaining. The alternative is merely an endless series of incomplete explanations. Rational beings, says the believer, are committed to the search for the most complete understanding of things precisely because they are rational, so they will not be satisfied with such incompleteness. This, say the believers, favours their position because God would provide the necessary completeness if he indeed exists.

The argument before us is obviously not a proof that God exists. But believers think it helps their case by showing that theism represents a higher level of rational commitment than the kind of 'I don't know' or agnostic attitude so fashionable in secularist circles. It suggests that if there is a God, then there is also an answer to the question about why anything exists at all, and it would also imply that God gave us minds capable of asking that question and sensing its importance as a way of letting us find our own way to a sense of his existence as 'the beginning and end of all things and of rational creatures especially', as Thomas Aquinas, the great thirteenth-century philosophical theologian, once said.

In short, believers argue that it is intellectually irresponsible to rest content without the best and fullest possible explanation for things; that the universe itself seems to contain only things which cannot give us that explanation; and that the concept of God indicates something that would answer it very richly indeed and in a way that befits human dignity. Coupled with additional arguments to be given below, which believers think show that God is no mere concept but utterly real, this somewhat abstract, philosophical argument about ultimate explanation provides an important opening strategy for the believer by revealing that the God-question is not just something that arises from the facts about Christ but also arises from (and could well be the only answer to) the most basic question any thinking being could ask.

The second philosophical argument based on the nature of the cosmos contends that if anything is to exist at all, a single God is more likely than the universe with all its complexities. The argument uses a philosophical principle to the effect that the simpler something is, the more likely it is, all other things being equal. For example, if we are faced with two equally plausible explanations of the same historical event like the outbreak of a war, resting on equal evidence, one of which is simpler than the other, then we would logically prefer the simpler. This is one reason why most thinking people are sceptical about conspiracy theories of history, which see things like secret committees of super-rich men at work behind the scenes to manipulate human affairs, in addition to all the usual factors discussed by historians. We may be unable to refute these theories but most of us find them superfluous because they add an unnecessary complexity to historical explanation. Similarly, simple situations are inherently more to be expected than complex ones containing more components or problems. For example, it is much more likely that the leaves falling from a tree will not form a pattern on the ground (in other words, be very unorganized or 'simple') than that they will form a neat triangle or a letter of the alphabet – and thus be highly organized or complex.

Philosophers speak here of the greater 'prior probability' of the simple over the complex. This principle logically means that the greatest prior probability exists for whatever has the greatest simplicity, other things being equal. Oxford philosopher of religion Richard Swinburne has argued impressively in his book *The Existence of God* that a deity like the one believed in by Christians, who is described as a completely unified, perfectly harmonious, single being possessing infinite powers, and who would thus be an exceedingly simple kind of entity, is more likely to exist than something less simple than he, all other things being equal. For example, such a God is more to be expected than many gods (which involves greater complexity than monotheism) or than a single God with only a certain amount of power, because there is less to explain in the notion of infinite power than in the notion of a specific amount of power. The same, says Swinburne, applies to a highly complex thing like our cosmos.

The argument before us is highly abstract, so let me try to present it as simply as possible. As rational people we would never ignore any problem that calls for explanation, for to do so is the mark of the unthinking person, not the thinker. Among the countless problems that puzzle us and trigger off a search for explanations, there is this universe of ours with its obvious complexity. So we ask, why does this complex universe of which we are part exist at all? Now some people merely shrug their shoulders and reply that there is no explanation for the universe. It is just a brute, mysterious fact. But as Swinburne points out, that doesn't seem a very rational answer, because a bit of thought reveals that complex things cry out for explanation precisely because they are complex. If anything qualifies as a brute fact, it is logically more likely to be something simple, especially something that is as simple as possible. That is a far cry from the nature of our universe. So, the believer continues, rationality itself makes us reject the idea that our complex universe must just be accepted as a brute, unexplained fact. In theory it could be so, but the odds are logically against such a theory, just as we find ourselves being logically sceptical that the leaves from a tree could drop into a figure 8 all on their own as a brute, uncaused fact of nature. Our minds rebel against such an unlikely theory and turn instead to the search for an explanation.

In connection with the universe this means returning to our opening question of why this universe of ours exists. And if we recall the philosophical argument given earlier in this section, which argues that everything in the universe seems to have a cause, then our question can hardly be answered by pointing to anything in the universe itself. That leaves us with a proposed cause beyond the universe, such as some kind of non-physical power, for instance one or more gods. And of these, a single, perfectly unified deity is logically the most likely.

The kalam argument fits very well into the believer's case at this point. It uses the principle that it is impossible to cross an actual infinite, like counting to infinity. But if the universe were eternal and thus had existed infinitely, then the present moment could never be reached. To get here one would have to cross an actual infinite, as J.P. Moreland puts it in the book *Does God Exist? The Great Debate*, but that is impossible. Since we obviously are here, it follows that the universe must have had a beginning. In other words, it came into existence at a certain instant in the past. This raises the question how it came into existence, and there are two possible answers. Either it happened spontaneously out of nothing, or it was made to happen out of nothing by something which exists independently. The only independent thing capable of causing something as vast, complex and highly structured as the universe to come into existence is a God who has unimaginably vast powers of mind and creation, such as the God believed in by monotheists.

Which of these two possibilities is more likely? Since experience is our best guide despite being imperfect (as David Hume pointed out over two hundred years ago); since experience shows that everything we encounter has a cause; and since we are rationally entitled to trust our experience unless there are good grounds to do otherwise (as with mirages), it is extremely hard to believe, says the theist, that the cosmos simply happened out of nothing. Creation by a God would be much more rationally believable, especially when considered in the light of the two previous arguments in this section.

Taken together, then, these abstract philosophical arguments about the cosmos and its cause (if any) do not on their own *prove* that God exists. But, says the believer, they show that the God-theory is rationally very impressive and enjoys much greater prior or intrinsic probability than its secular rival in this opening round of argument. If the remaining evidence for such a God proves equally impressive, then the total argument would clearly favour the believer.

Physics and God

The favourite science for many modern Christians arguing in favour of belief in God is physics. I referred to it in my opening chapter; now it is necessary to present this physics-based argument more fully. As a preliminary step Christians point out that the founding fathers of classical or pre-quantum physics like Copernicus, Galileo, Kepler and Newton were all firmly convinced about the existence of God, just as many of today's modern physicists are theists too. That there are as many others – and maybe more – who are not believers is of course also a fact, but the point is that there is no inherent link between physics and atheism or non-theistic ways of viewing the cosmos.

The main argument, however, is that the picture of the universe unfolded by the latest advances in physics makes the God-hypothesis more likely to be correct than its rivals. Most scientists now support the so-called 'big bang' theory, though this may be subject to review in the light of recent deep red-shift surveys. This theory says that the universe as we know it began when an immensely compressed fireball exploded, hurling its energy outward. This event is thought to have happened about eighteen billion years ago. As the energy exploded outward, increasing the volume it occupied, so it cooled to ever-lower temperatures. In the merest fractions of a second after that fiery birth of the cosmos, this fall in temperature enabled the elements to form – the lightest ones first while the heavy elements like iron and gold were formed later in supernovae, until all the natural elements had formed. Later on in the same process came the birth of galaxies and individual stars like our sun, all of them rushing outwards from the point of the big bang itself. And much, much later, cooling fragments from the fiery substance of those stars provided the raw materials for the next great stage of this mighty process, the birth of planets like our own. Thus there formed this still-expanding, still-cooling universe of ours, and in a particular corner of it our own solar system and our own home planet, born about four billion years ago.

But the crucial final touch in this piece of exciting scientific thought – technically called 'cosmology' because it theorizes about the story of the whole cosmos – is that from the instant of the big bang onwards, everything was present in precisely the one way, among many other possible ways, that makes it possible for us as thinking human beings to be here today discussing matters like this. Had things been even slightly different in the condition of that original fireball fifteen billion years ago, we would not here. The chemical make-up of our bodies and brains depends on a very complex, highly precise arrangement of the structure of matter and energy themselves. Had things not been exactly as they were – had they taken any of the countless other forms that are mathematically possible – then the big bang would have produced a different kind of universe, perhaps a dead-end universe without the conditions needed for life to emerge. We would then not have been here today to study the stars and ourselves. But we *are* here – offspring of a fireball that was precisely right to give us birth against incredible odds. It is as if things contained a massive bias in favour of intelligent life from the very beginning, rather than any of the multitude of other kinds of bias that were possible.

At this point big bang cosmology becomes immensely important for all of us who wrestle with the God-question today. It makes us keenly aware of two key questions which previous generations could not have asked : where did the original fireball which exploded fifteen billion years ago come from, and how did it come about that it contained within itself such an incredible, odds-against bias in favour of the emergence of intelligent life?

So far as we can see, there are in the end just two possible answers to both questions; either nature or God. If nature alone is the answer, then the original fireball must either have arisen on its own out of nothing (so that reality as a whole would have begun to exist at that point, with absolutely nothing prior to it, not even time) or the fireball arose from a previous phase – perhaps a contracting phase – in the story of a universe which has no beginning or end. Both of those are purely natural explanations of the source of the cosmos. And as for the second question, the naturalistic answer is that the fireball, and thus reality itself, just happened to have that incredible life-bias all on its own.

The God-answer to this problem comes from religion but it can just as easily arise from science. If naturalistic explanations turn out to have their own problems, then scientific curiosity will begin to look for others. Most scientists so far appear to favour the view that things actually began with the big bang, rather than the view that the universe is eternal. So far as the source of the original fireball is concerned, this means looking for a cause which must have within itself the mind-boggling power to produce that fireball out of nothing, a fireball in which all the energy of the entire universe was compressed. A God would meet this requirement, because the word 'God' in this context means a being with infinite power. Making a universe out of nothing might strike us as impossible but it would not be beyond the power of an infinitely mighty being. (Energy and mass are inter-convertible, so in physical terms to make a universe out of nothing – that is, out of no other matter having mass – is not a theoretical problem as long as the energy was available from which to create the mass of the universe.)

Believers in God see here a powerful indication that things point more rationally towards God as the answer than to the alternative. But this is by far not their main argument, and if physics were to show that the universe is probably without a beginning, then believers in God would still have their main point in hand. And this concerns the second of the questions posed above, namely the explanation for the incredible life-bias that was present in our universe at the time of the big bang. Believers argue that the thinking, open-minded person must choose between the idea that the life-bias is just an extremely unlikely brute fact, or that it points to the presence of something which intended that there should be a life-producing cosmos, and had the power to design and produce it. The only thing which could combine intention, design and such mighty production is a conscious mind which possesses virtually infinite power, and that is precisely what believers mean when they speak of God as the creator of the universe.

Which explanation is more likely? Trading heavily on the massive unlikelihood that a life-giving universe could have happened as an accident of nature, believers conclude, in words from Cambridge theologian Brian Hebblethwaite's book *The Ocean of Truth*, that the universe, by contrast, is indicative of intention. Using modern physics, they say it gives good grounds for preferring the God-explanation to its rival. That, they say, makes belief in God more rational in this respect at least than naturalism. And they go on to point out that if we add the force of the biological argument which will be discussed next, then it becomes even more rational to favour God above nature as the real explanation for the intricate web of life that has come about in this fiery, expanding universe. When told that many scientists – perhaps most – today are agnostics or even atheists, they reply that this is mainly because the hostility which the church showed to people like Galileo and Darwin made the scientific community deeply suspicious of religion, and not because of any real clash between science and belief in God.

Biology and God

That biology should offer grounds for belief in God might seem surprising because of the clash between biblical creationists and Darwinian evolutionists. This has created the impression that biology runs counter to theism. That was certainly the picture of things for a century after the appearance of Darwin's famous book *The Origin*

50

of Species in 1859. But more recent developments in biological science have been hailed by many Christians as providing important new grounds for their faith in God. Molecular biology in particular has revealed not only the enormous diversity of the forms of life but also their incredible complexity, making it extremely difficult to believe, say Christians, that a purely natural process of random or chance changes in the genetic make-up of organisms – caused, for example, by changes in the radiation reaching the earth from space – could plausibly explain that incredible complexity in the available amount of time since the alleged beginnings of life on earth roughly 3000 million years ago.

The argument is thus that the God-hypothesis makes better sense than the nature-alone theory of the secularists to the effect that life evolved by chance, because the former can easily explain the complexity in the given time-span of life on earth – or in much less time for that matter. A God with an infinite mind and limitless power can obviously design and implement a creation scenario such as the story of life on earth as unfolded by modern biology. A vivid example of the problem facing naturalistic biology in this regard is given by Richard Hazelett and Dean Turner in their recent book *Benevolent Living*, citing Michael Denton's book *Evolution: A Theory in Crisis*, pp. 327f. Denton uses the example of a single, living cell magnified in the imagination a thousand million times so that it is twenty kilometres in diameter, like some gigantic airship hovering over a large city. It is worth quoting him in full:

What we would then see would be an object of unparalleled complexity and adaptive design. On the surface of the cell we would see millions of openings, like the port holes of a vast space ship, opening and closing to allow a continual stream of materials to flow in and out. If we were to enter one of these openings we would find ourselves in world of supreme technology and bewildering complexity. Is it really credible that random processes could have constructed a reality, the smallest element of which – a functional protein or gene – is complex beyond our own creative capacities . . . ?

The point being made is that we humans – the most intelligent beings on earth – cannot remotely match even this elementary level of biological complexity in our own handiwork, which makes it utterly improbable that mindless, natural forces acting by chance could have done so, especially in the limited time available. And if there are problems with a naturalistic, chance-based explanation of the level of complexity present in a single cell, imagine how much greater the problems are with even more complex phenomena like the human eye, not to speak of the whole, interconnected web of life.

To dramatize the point, theists sometimes say that a purely naturalistic explanation of life on earth is therefore about as likely as a monkey in front of a typewriter or word-processor producing *Macbeth*. They therefore conclude that only people with a prior commitment to opposing theism – in other words, bigots – could insist on so manifestly improbable an explanation for the presence of life on earth. And if naturalistic accounts prove to be that improbable, then the rational step is to incline towards a supernatural account. Since this, in turn, requires the presence of a force both massively powerful and intelligent, the only kind of supernatural cause that fits the bill is a creator God.

Thoughtful, informed Christians thus conclude that philosophy, physics and biology provide independent, rational reasons for thinking that there probably is a God. These reasons, in turn, fuse with the conclusions they reach from their study of the facts about Jesus of Nazareth, namely that he probably did rise from the dead and that our best explanation for that event is not that there are hidden, death-defying natural powers within a few highly gifted individuals (though that is possible), but that there truly is a God with death-defying powers who set the mighty seal of his approval on the life and message of Jesus. Surely, they ask, any reasonable, fair-minded person can see that this blend of arguments from the New Testament, from philosophy, physics and from biology is already strong enough to show that there probably is a God of infinite love, goodness and power – a God memorably described by Brian Hebblethwaite as 'the source and power of the world, of history, and of our own life as creatures . . . the infinite Creator of the world's, including our own, whole being, God, the source of all value, God, present in our own

midst in both incarnation and inspiration, God, who, it is
will in the end take his fragile personal creation, transfori
the conditions of eternity to know and enjoy him for ever' (*The
Ocean of Truth*, pp.6, 4).

The objective evidence: 3. Philosophical anthropology

Human nature

We move on now to arguments based on various facts about
humanity. Believers point to certain important aspects of human
nature and argue that these either imply that a God would be the
best explanation for them, or are so hard to explain on purely physical
terms that they undermine confidence in non-theistic philosophies.
Not surprisingly, these arguments all relate to our mental life, broadly
considered, for that is what allegedly lifts us above the level of other
animals and enables us to ponder ultimate questions concerning our
source and destiny, if any. I shall mention the three most important
arguments of this kind.

Firstly, our capacity for advanced knowledge, which is marvellously matched to the orderly structures of the universe, is said to be
improbable if chance alone governed the way humanity has evolved,
but is just what one would expect if a loving God exists, for he can
be expected to create beings with minds capable of understanding
and appreciating the universe and wondering why it exists. The
cosmos is intelligible to us precisely because our incredibly complex
thinking equipment is such as to be able to unlock its secrets,
and thereby advance from scientific to philosophical and religious
knowledge of the kind dealt with above when we considered the
philosophical arguments for the existence of God. Secondly, the
same argument is sometimes also used in connection with our self-
transcending abilities as humans. This means our constant reaching
out for something better than we already have or already are. Athletes,
for example, strive endlessly to improve their own performances and
break old records. Scientists and thinkers do the same in the field of
knowledge, forever researching new puzzles or seeking better ways
of understanding things. This is in marked contrast with even the

most intelligent of the other species on our planet, like chimpanzees or dolphins, which have remained very much where they began, constantly repeating the same pattern of life from generation to generation. Progress among humans may be uneven but it does take place, at least in some activities, yet it is quite absent elsewhere in the animal kingdom.

Thus we humans strive for something better, strive to surpass or transcend what we already have and are. Many believers see here an important sign that we have been made to reach out beyond ourselves by a loving creator. The famous Christian thinker of the early church, St Augustine of Hippo in North Africa, captured this idea perfectly in a prayer which goes as follows: 'O God, Thou has made us for Thyself and our hearts are restless until they rest in Thee.' Nobody thinks that this proves that there is a God. The point being made, rather, is that our human nature in these respects fits well into the believer's picture of things. By contrast, there are atheists who have noted the same human qualities but, finding no God in whom to believe as our source and goal, conclude that human existence is absurd and meaningless because it is equipped for a God who simply isn't there. Believers suggest that the very absurdity of such a situation makes it unlikely to be true in a universe where everything else fits so neatly together. Why should that neatness in the rest of nature suddenly evaporate in connection with human nature?

Another argument used by believers is based on the fact of consciousness in humans and, evidently, in some animals. Materialists, for whom the basic or even only reality is matter, say that all talk about consciousness or minds can be translated into talk about brains and brain-events. But this is easier said than done, and many thoughtful people conclude that mental reality is not identical with physical reality. Wishes, desires, thoughts and other aspects of consciousness seem very different from physical things which can be perceived by the senses, weighed, and counted. This leads them to believe that people (and perhaps some animals) are a union of two parts, their bodies and their minds (or rational souls, in religious terms). That raises the key question of the origin of the mind/soul, since it has not been satisfactorily explained as a product of physical evolution going back to the big bang. Believers once again find that there is something messy and incomplete about materialistic theories, whereas the God-theory gives a perfectly smooth and logical explanation for the fact of consciousness by seeing its source as God. That adds to the probability that there is a God, though no thinking believer would say it proves his existence.

Religion and God

The arguments we have just reviewed flow naturally into the next step in the believer's case, which holds that the existence of religion as a fact of human history also points us to God as its most likely cause. Experts confirm that religion is a feature of every known society on earth, past and present. As Wilfred Cantwell Smith, the eminent Canadian historian of religions has said, faith is the human rule and secularism the exception. Studies also show that while there are important religions like Buddhism, Chinese religion and parts of Hinduism which find no need for the notion of a God (as understood in this book), nonetheless most religions have that notion. Belief in spiritual beings presided over by a senior or supreme being is very nearly what scholars call a 'cultural universal', meaning that it is found in virtually all cultures.

Now it is vital to grasp that one need not be in the least religious to make this point about the world-wide scope of belief in a God, for it is a matter of fact, not an item of religious teaching, just as the complexity of the living cell or the structures studied by physics are matters of fact, not of faith. But given the facts about belief in God in practically every human society, the question that then arises is what this means. Why is theism so widespread, and atheism (or non-theistic religion) the exception? Why has a majority of the human race always believed that there is a God, even in our own, secular-seeming culture?

Once again there seems to be just two basic, possible explanations. Either there is no God at all, so that the concept of a supreme being has arisen as an invention of the human mind, or there is indeed a God corresponding more or less closely to the ideas people have of him. If faith in God is merely a human invention with no basis in fact, then it is obviously a delusion. But how likely is that? How likely, asks the believer, is it that the bulk of the human race throughout history has been deluded? For that to be in the least bit credible we need some extremely impressive explanations – and believers think that their critics have failed dismally to give these, as we shall shortly see. That makes it more logical, they say, to regard God as the probable explanation for God-orientated religion.

According to the most impressive Christian version of this theistic explanation of religion, our ideas about God have come about as a result of two processes both of which have him as their ultimate source. One of these is human creativity. Here people's minds form the God-idea on their own, using the powers of thought which God of course enabled them to have by creating this kind of life-giving cosmos. This means that God equips us to find our own way to him. The other alleged process comes more directly from God when he reveals himself to the great prophets and holy people and in the great scriptures of the world, giving humanity a clearer picture of his nature and purpose. Christians have traditionally seen this second process of divine revelation in the prophets of ancient Israel, in the writing of the Bible and above all in its final, complete form in Jesus Christ. But nowadays there are increasing numbers of Christians who believe that God has given evidence of himself much more widely than this as the inspiring force behind all the great religious teachers of the world, or at least behind all who believe in a God. For example, the Roman Catholic theologian Hans Küng has recently argued that Christians must acknowledge that Muhammad, the founding prophet of Islam, is indeed a true prophet of God.

So we find ourselves having to ask what is more likely, that religion and especially all God-believing religion is a mere human invention, a contagious delusion in a godless universe, or whether it is a varied but basically sound response by humanity to the God whose invisible, loving presence enfolds all things. Christians naturally focus this question on Christ. They ask which is more likely – that the Jesus who spoke with such inner conviction of his powerful awareness of the Heavenly Father, backing up that message with a life of self-sacrificing love, was in fact in touch with reality, or that he was deluded or even dishonest? (This is of course the famous so-called trilemma, to the effect that Jesus was either God, mad or bad.) And they conclude that no rational person can seriously dismiss Jesus as dishonest or deluded, because of the goodness, mental clarity and manifest sanity of his life in every other respect. This doesn't give us a mathematically certain proof that he was genuinely in direct contact with God as his Father, they argue, but it makes that view more likely than its non-theistic rivals. And in a lesser way, progressive Christians make the same point about all the other seemingly God-filled religious teachers and sacred books.

Essentially, believers are saying that these people gave rise to and shaped all the great God-believing religions of the world. They were people of the greatest moral stature and their teachings in general have a beauty and inspiring quality for billions of people in all parts of the world, with an influence lasting thousands of years. Is it really credible that all of this is sheer delusion? Isn't it more likely that secularism, with vastly fewer followers and a much shorter history, is the delusion?

Ironically, Christians (and other theists) argue that they are assisted rather than refuted at this point by the three most famous naturalistic attempts at explaining religion, those by Feuerbach, Marx and Freud. They argue that these are all severely flawed. It is important that we note the faults they find with the work of these famous critics of religion.

Ludwig Feuerbach was a German thinker of the mid-nineteenth century. His famous book *The Essence of Christianity* (published in German in 1841) tries to show that belief in God is the product of what we would call an unconscious human process of projecting an ideal image of ourselves outwards, so creating the concept of God. But in fact there is no such being, said Feuerbach, only ourselves and our highest moral ideals which we transfer on to that imaginary God. This makes anthropology – the study of humanity – the true basis and clue to the real meaning of theology. Feuerbach's work is detailed and rich with insight as he explains his own version of the supposed essence of Christianity. But the main line of argument is the theory that we humans create the image of God out of ourselves and not because we correctly (though also dimly) perceive the presence of a God who exists independently of us. We create God in our own best image, not the other way around as Christians and other believers in God suppose.

Believers reply to all this by pointing out that Feuerbach's theory may show us the *process* by which people since ancient times have formed their ideas about invisible, personal, spiritual beings. But that doesn't itself mean that there is no God. It is perfectly possible that God exists and created a universe containing a planet on which intelligent creatures emerged, equipped with minds capable of forming the God-concept on their own by means of the mental process discussed by Feuerbach. Feuerbach's atheistic standpoint needs a further, separate argument showing that in all probability there is no God, but he gives no such argument. Instead, he confuses psychology of religion (the study of mental and behavioural aspects of religion) with philosophy of religion (which includes arguments for and against belief in God), and merely assumes that theism is false. But that begs the question in his own favour – a well-known error of reasoning. Thus believers can validly object that Feuerbach's projection theory can as easily be used to show how the mind finds its way to its maker, as to show how the mind invents the alleged fiction of having a maker. This seriously damages his work as a naturalistic explanation of belief in God.

Marx read Feuerbach's book as a young man and believed that Feuerbach had settled the God-question against the believer. He then focussed his attention on the way religion all around him functioned in society, and saw it, famously, as the opium of the people – a pain-killing drug that deadens people to the pain of their exploited, needlessly suffering existence, above all in capitalist countries. But the value of this theory is the way it exposes the *abuse* of faith in a God who, so it is believed, will in the end make everything right, an abuse practised by people in power who want others to be submissive in the face of injustice. While this valuably unmasks a serious social evil, it offers little to explain why belief in God arose in the first place, because we know such belief to have been present in societies which are free of the economic exploitation Marx correctly detested. Nor does it explain why faith in God continues to be widespread in the world's richest and most egalitarian societies. Besides, Marx gave the matter only the most minimal attention. His few, brief passages about religion are vividly written but fall far short of a detailed explanation of faith in God, for Marx believed that Feuerbach had satisfactorily shown the human origins of religion, and we have also already seen that believers have no trouble in robbing Feuerbach's main argument of most of its force. Marx's theory of religion may help us grasp something of the grim reality of impoverished factory workers, but is unable to cast helpful light on Jesus or Paul (or Moses and Muhammed, for that matter) and their innumerable followers whose lives are not made bearable merely by a Sunday dose of spiritual opium.

Things are only slightly better, say Christians, with Freud's notion that faith in God is a neurotic illusion created and accepted unconsciously by the human mind as a comfort against the pain and dread which would cripple us if we actually faced up to the facts of our existence. According to this view, the hard facts are that we are on our own in a universe which is entirely unaware of and unconcerned about us. When we die, that is the end for us. But very few people, said Freud, are capable of the realism of facing these alleged facts. Instead we typically and universally seek comfort in the belief that there is a God out there who can overcome the frailties of this mortal existence of ours, a God we unconsciously invent on the model of our own fathers because they are our best example of a strong, protecting, sometimes stern figure.

Freud offered his view of religion in a famous and eloquent book called *The Future of an Illusion*, and his great influence on psychology and especially psycho-analysis has ensured a wide influence for his ideas. But they break no really new ground when one recalls the theories of Feuerbach and Marx. Between them those two earlier thinkers worked out the ideas of human projection in the face of suffering, resulting allegedly in delusions about a God out there who looks after us, ideas which are basic to Freud's theory as well. What he changed was the nature of the suffering. Marx found it in economic exploitation; Freud saw it (correctly) as much more widespread than that. He recognized that suffering is part and parcel of human existence anywhere – a recognition, incidentally, which he shares with the Buddha. He is obviously correct here. And many believers do indeed seek refuge from life's storms in the God they think cares everlastingly for us all. But that is a motive for believing, not a proof that there is no God, especially not a God who is found through suffering. Furthermore, it is asking far too much of informed people to accept that all the great thinkers of history who believed in God – including the founding fathers of physics and mathematics like Newton, Leibniz and Pascal – were emotional weaklings neurotically in need of a night-light for their anxious souls.

As these accounts of our main naturalistic theories of religion show, believers are entitled to say that their own case, resting as it does on strongly factual appeals to history and science, is not much weakened by such opposition, which consistently confuses psychological and sociological studies of the way believers form their ideas (valuable though these are in their own right) with proper arguments for and against the claim that God exists. How some people become believers – indeed, how all believers reach their convictions – is quite distinct from whether or not their faith is valid or deluded. Accordingly, Christians feel entirely justified on rational grounds in dismissing the classical naturalistic theories of religion as fatally flawed, and believe that this swings the balance of probability firmly in their favour as far as the real cause of religion is concerned.

But why then do some major religions manage without any notion of a God as defined in this book? Why did so saintly, noble and intelligent a person as the Buddha, to name but one, find no need for that concept? Even if these people are a minority, we still need a plausible explanation from Christians and other God-believing people for their seeming blindness to the existence of God. Very few theists give this problem much attention. Of those who do, some offer problematic answers while others offer more plausible answers. We will note briefly the former but concentrate on the latter.

The problematic theories are that these non-theistic religious believers are deceived by the ever-wily devil, or are themselves stubborn and blind. Nobody who studies the facts with an open mind could accept these proposals. Other theists therefore offer different explanations. They argue that people like the Buddha are indeed great spiritual and ethical figures but that they took what have turned out with hindsight to be blind alleys in their quest for the truth, just as science contains examples of noble people whose theories proved, in the end, mistaken. Many leading scientists once preferred the phlogiston theory of why things burn, now known to be mistaken, to the now-accepted oxygenation theory, and there were physicists in the nineteenth century who mistakenly thought that 'aether' was a valid scientific concept.

Another factor that is said to explain their supposed error without demeaning them is cultural conditioning. All of us are strongly influenced by our cultures. Even truly great religious leaders who grow up far from the places where the God-concept is strongest will inevitably be at a disadvantage compared to others. Some of them, understandably, will strike out in a different direction as they seek the truth about the great questions of life, because none of the best guides are available, just as very few people in the former USSR until recently will have really appreciated that a free society works better than a controlled system. Under the pressure of massive cultural conditioning they can hardly be expected to do otherwise. The same, we are told, holds good for religion. This then gives us an adequate explanation for the minority of believers whose faith has no room in it for the concept of God. And as a final touch, those who argue like this sometimes add that in any case the concept of God is philosophically more impressive than its religious rivals. All of this is then said to square very well with the larger numbers of God-believers because it is more likely that the theistic majority is correct than the minority, all other things being at least equal, which they are.

The conclusion reached, obviously, is that God-orientated religion is sounder than its rivals. The explanation does not sneer at or demean the non-theists. It sees them as impressive, honourable figures who proceeded honestly but still mistakenly. And it adds the further point that in all the so-called non-theistic religions we find, in fact, that something very much like the concept of a personal God always finds its way back into those religions, as if the truth must prevail. Thus many Buddhists give devotion to Lord Amidha as a heavenly saviour and more Hindus, so it is said, worship Lord Krishna than meditate about an allegedly non-theistic conception of the ultimate reality such as Brahman.

This way of explaining why a minority of the world's believers finds no need for the concept of God will not work for Christians who insist that the truth about God comes to us from God himself by means of revelation alone. That insistence leads to the fatal question why God failed to show the truth to some of his needy children. Why did he reveal the truth to Moses, Isaiah and Jesus, and maybe (for some Christians anyway) also to Muhammed or the Guru Nanak – but not a word of it to the Buddha, Lao Tze and Confucius? Such behaviour smacks of unfair dealing and thus contradicts the perfect goodness of God, so thinking Christians cannot argue like that. Their best policy really is to emphasize the human search for truth and thus argue that this search takes various paths, some fruitful, others less so, in religion as in science – along the lines summarized above. This certainly means that some forms of theism are more rational and moral than others. But the existence of incomplete or even crude forms of God-religion is no more a disproof of God's existence than crude ideas about science in some places proves that black holes are a myth.

What about Judaism, Islam, the monotheistic parts of Hinduism and all other religions which believe there is one God? For informed, sensitive Christians, any religion which teaches that there is one God only must be regarded as sound in that respect. The same holds for a belief in the perfect goodness and almighty power of God, which those other monotheisms also teach. The key issue here is not monotheism but Jesus Christ. No other monotheism, says the Christian, contains the truth about Christ. Islam honours and accepts Jesus as a true prophet but believes that Muhammad is the messenger through whom God's fullest truth has been spoken. For Christians this view, while acknowledged with respect, falls short of the facts which history, so they argue, forces us all to face – the facts that were discussed earlier in this chapter. Judaism, in order to be true to its own ancient teachings and to the God whom Israel faithfully served for thousands of years, cannot find a place in its doctrines for Jesus of Nazareth because of his departures from the sacred Torah or Law of Moses. Sensitive Christians, aware of the terrible anti-semitism their fellow believers have sometimes practised, find it painful to raise this matter, but nonetheless respond to this view by saying that in a rational debate it is the evidence that must lead us all, and that an open-minded study of the evidence about Jesus supports their view of him better than any other. And in a broadly similar way

Christians have no choice but to extend this point to all other monotheistic faiths, none of which offers a picture of Jesus Christ, according to Christians, which does justice to the historical evidence as summarized earlier in this chapter. That leads them to conclude that the fullest truth is to be found in the one monotheistic faith which does base itself on that historical evidence, namely Christianity.

Drawing these ideas together, we can now see why believers think that the facts about religion point us more strongly to the conclusion that the God whom Jesus of Nazareth spoke about exists in the first place as the eternal lure calling forth humanity's dominant religious response, than to either the naturalistic conclusion that everything without exception comes from nature, or to the alternative religious view that a spiritual reality other than God is at the heart of things. A parallel argument is also given concerning the moral element in human experience, and to that we must now proceed.

Goodness of life and God

We saw earlier in this chapter that Jesus of Nazareth not only spoke about a God of love but himself lived a life of love, even laying down his life for others. Believers also point out that a long and noble succession of others has shown a striking goodness of life, including martyrdom and other impressive levels of self-sacrifice. Sometimes scholars speak here of 'conspicuous sanctity', meaning a goodness and holiness of life that is moving and exceptional. And in a less dramatic way they also draw attention to the active concern for others revealed in countless Christian lives. Looking further afield, those open-minded Christians who know something about Jews, Muslims and other believers in God find that compassion and a high morality are also strongly present in those religions. Each of them, just like Christianity, calls on its followers to behave with a goodness that has its source, so they believe, in God.

Moving on from these facts of impressive, personal morality among believers – which I for one have often observed – the argument next draws our attention to the very different way of life encouraged by secular economic and political philosophies, where the accent so often falls on personal advantage and self-concern leading to exploitation, injustice and war. Nature itself is sometimes brought into the argument, because of the seemingly instinctive way we humans and many animals appear to be driven to take care of our own basic needs above all else. Considered merely as a blob of flesh, who of us, believers ask, would rather die of thirst than give our last cup of water to someone else, especially if that person is not a relative? Who of us would regularly deny ourselves a glass of our favourite wine in order to give a loaf of bread to the hungry? Yet that is something which countless believers in God have done and continue to do. Where do they get the strength and inspiration to live such better lives?

Wise theists know that there is no simple link between goodness of life and faith in God. They know that faith doesn't turn everybody into a Mother Teresa. But they also argue that faith produces moral transformation often enough to make it reasonable to suppose that the change has something to do with the loving power of God which they believe he freely makes available to all who want it. Believers cannot claim that this is a proof of God's existence, least of all on its own. But they can and do say that it fits well into their cumulative case. After all, if the kind of God they believe in really does exist, then his loving presence is real everywhere. One would then expect that people who sincerely open their lives to it would be changed for the better when that power flows into their lives – like being invigorated by some breaths of fresh air after a long meeting in a stuffy room. And that, they say, is what happens to all who truly love and serve God. Their own move into greater goodness of life thus confirms and deepens their faith, and is offered to the enquirer and the sceptic as further evidence that God is indeed real.

Miracles

Some believers are uncomfortable with the argument from miracles, defined as events which no human or natural force known to us could cause. But there really is no getting away from miracles for mainline Christians, as we saw earlier in this chapter, because the birth of their religion (and that of Judaism and Islam) involves what can be seen as founding miracles like the crossing of the Red Sea by the children of Israel under Moses, the raising of the dead Jesus, and the revealing of Islam's sacred scriptures, the Holy Qur'an. Muslims regard this as an event which no human could have produced. Moreover, there is no shortage of reports about miracles in our own day and age, especially miracles of healing. Thus a priest comes to the bedside of a dying child, prays to God through Christ for healing, and the child recovers. Many of us know about incidents like this, and may even have observed or been involved in them ourselves. In the Roman Catholic Church there are reportedly officials whose task is to screen alleged miracles very meticulously, which they do. But despite the care taken to exclude anything that is mistaken (or worse), still there are some events which this process finds authentic.

What is one to make of all this, asks the believer? One can act the bigot and refuse even to consider the possibility of miracles, but we are not interested in arguing with bigots, however learned, clever and refined. (Believers are well aware that bigotry is not always vulgar or obtuse. Sometimes it is subtle and persuasive, preferring mild chuckles of condescension and dry cynicism to a blunt refusal to look at evidence.) By contrast, really open-minded people will look at anything that might count as evidence, and they will be especially aware that their own convictions could be mistaken. Such people will concede, however reluctantly, that events take place from time to time which seem to be far beyond any human power to produce. And once this key point is admitted, then the same question arises which we have met before in this chapter: what causes these events? And the same basic options must again be weighed against each other – either God or something else, including human effort, of a kind we do not yet understand.

Believers often argue wrongly at this point. They conclude that miracles prove beyond doubt that God exists. This is incorrect. To argue this way merely makes it easy for sceptics to refute them. Things are more subtle and much less certain than that, for the correct conclusion is that while some unknown natural or purely human power may indeed be the real cause of miracles, it is also possible that God is the real cause, provided there are other valid reasons for believing in him. As we have seen, Christians have a seemingly impressive, mounting case based on biblical history, philosophy, physics, biology and religion itself in favour of the conclusion that God does indeed exist. What is more, he has the character of love, and would thus want to help people in ways which his infinite mind knowns to be best, puzzling though this may be to us with our limited minds. Therefore miracles are to be expected from time to time when people who love and trust God call on him for help according to his will, and that is exactly what happens, says the believer. Miracles fit logically into the way we would expect things to work if God exists. Surely this is a more reasonable conclusion than some vague (though logically possible) notion that unknown natural or even supernatural forces are responsible?

The argument has two levels of strength, and wise believers know better than to confuse them. One of them applies to open-minded people debating the existence of God at a theoretical level. The most the believer can expect here is to show that genuine cases of healing or some other benefit, cases which defy ordinary explanation, could indeed be the work of a caring God and do fit logically into the believer's world-view, and then add these two considerations to their main pillars of argument. The second level concerns anybody who may have personal experience of an inexplicable healing or the like taking place after prayer. Here things will be experienced quite differently, with a vividness and power which no outsider debating these things at second or third hand can be expected to feel. At this level miracles will naturally seem like compelling proof to the few people who experience them. But for the greater number who do not, much less can be achieved by appealing to miracles, though this does not make the appeal pointless. It too, says the thoughtful theist, has its place in showing that the case for the believer is comprehensive, logical and persuasive. This way of approaching miracles ends up achieving more than the exaggerated, simplistic claims of some believers who wrongly think that the appeal to miracles is a simple and decisive remedy for scepticism.

The objective evidence: 4. Experiences of God's presence

The last kind of evidence in the believer's case is the fact that many people have personal experiences which seem to be of a divine presence. As well as qualifying as objective evidence, religious experience must also be understood as giving the believer a very deep personal or subjective assurance about the truth of his or her faith. As such it amounts to a different kind of evidence from the various arguments we have so far been discussing. All of these started with facts which anybody can in principle check, whereas the inner experience of people is private. Because of this dual aspect of religious experience, as both objective in its way yet obviously also subjective, the present section will discuss both.

While miracles involve dramatic, baffling events which could be observed or filmed by investigators, religious experience is different. The Christians who have it report being aware of an invisible power affecting them in some way or other that is to their benefit, for example, helping them cope with a problem. To them there is no doubt that this invisible power is God, often experienced as the divine Christ or as the Holy Spirit. Easily the most famous of these experiences is the one that the New Testament says befell St Paul on the road to Damascus. An account of this event is given in chapter 9 of the Acts of the Apostles, where we read that a light suddenly flashed from the sky all around Paul (then still called Saul). He fell to the ground and heard a voice addressing him by name, claiming to be the selfsame Jesus whose followers were saying that he had risen from the dead. As a result Paul was blind for three days, and was converted from being a leading persecutor of the early Christians into a dedicated and forceful member of the new faith. Our historically best evidence for this incident comes in Paul's own letters, where he alludes to having seen Christ himself. While the details of the event are open to question, there can be no gainsaying that Paul had an experience which he was certain had revealed the risen Christ to him personally. And now in our own time we find many other Christians reporting similar experiences.

Early in this century in the USA William Starbuck and William James pioneered the psychological study of this phenomenon. More recently the British zoologist Alister Hardy did important follow-up work in Britain. He appealed through the press for first-hand reports of experiences of a higher power, and ended up with a collection of several thousand. Other writers who have studied this phenomenon, like David Hay in his book *Exploring Inner Space*, say that these experiences are less rare than our secular society might expect.

Having examined a selection of about 700 of the reports in Hardy's collection at Oxford, and having done a similar but small-scale pilot project of my own in South Africa, I have no doubt that these experiences are a fact. Here is an extract from a fairly typical report, taken from Hardy's book *The Spiritual Nature of Man* (p. 41):

> About 20 odd years ago I was rather poorly and one evening felt so ill that I decided to go to bed. While in my room preparing I suddenly felt all around me a beautiful warm Presence so comforting that I said out loud 'Well Father if I have to be ill to feel *you* like that – I will be ill.' Then the room filled with triumphant music – so beautiful it conveyed to me that I had chosen aright . . .
>
> The most important part is that ever since then I have a sense of Peace – sometimes more, sometimes less, but I feel cared for and led.

Naturally, experiences like this cannot prove that there is a God. It is always possible that they are tricks of the mind and no more. But there can be no doubting their effect on the people who have them, which is greatly to deepen and strengthen their faith in Christ if it already exists, and to kindle it if it doesn't, as with St Paul – especially if the experience is repeated. And when these people show no sign of mental disturbance whatsoever, they will be entitled to accept the experience at face value rather than suspect that their minds are misleading them. Thus believers who have had experiences like this will naturally find them the most vivid confirmation of or basis for their faith. It is most important to note at this point that believers are acting quite rationally in so doing, because there is every justification, as thinkers like John Hick and Richard Swinburne have pointed out, for people to accept that what seems to be the case, is the case, unless there are good reasons for thinking otherwise. If I have the experience of seeing what seems to be a tree, then surely I am justified in thinking that I am seeing one, and that it does exist. We could not function as thinking people if we did not, as a general rule, heed our experience. Why then should believers be denied the right to apply that principle to their religious experiences?

For people raised in a faith in God, religious experience can take a more pervasive form in addition to the dramatic kind we have been discussing. From very early in life they have accepted that God is the most basic and important of all realities. Bible study, worship and prayer enable them to develop a strong sense that God is the abiding foundation of their lives, so that everything that happens is interpreted in relation to that most central of convictions. They do not look around at nature or history and say, 'Ah, these things lead me to faith in God.' Just the reverse happens. They see these things *on the basis of their existing faith in God*. And they find that life works and makes sense when lived like this. The American philosopher of religion Alvin Plantinga has valuably drawn attention to the reality of these people's standpoint, for whom nothing is more basic than their sense of the presence of God. Given also that they are perfectly sane and decent people, what else can they rationally do but continue to live in accordance with their own deepest and most long-lasting experience, their sense of God's reality?

But even if we grant that this is a valid point, it is of doubtful value in the modern debate about God, because sceptics (and indeed other kinds of believer like Muslims and Buddhists) can just as validly say that they never have the slightest sense of a Christ-like divine presence, so they are equally rational when they reject Christianity. That seems to imply that conflicting world-views can be held with equal rational justification, which doesn't help those of us who find much to admire in both believers and sceptics, and who want to see if the dispute between them can be settled either way. We are not merely interested in what is rational; we want to know what is true.

Going back now to the more unusual kind of religious experience, we must note, next, that things are a bit different for believers in God who hear or read about these experiences without undergoing them for themselves. There will not be the direct, vivid, powerful confirmation felt by the recipient, but there will still be a sense that faith in God receives further validation from those experiences, because it fits the pattern. If a loving God really does exist, then there is nothing in the least odd about some people occasionally feeling his presence very clearly indeed. After all, he is there all the time, available, as it were, for encounter by our minds. When the mists of our human minds clear enough, the direct sunlight of his presence can be felt. Isn't that also precisely what Christianity teaches about the great prophets and biblical writers – that God came directly into their consciousness in order to reveal himself and his will? The difference between those landmark experiences and the kind reported by ordinary people is more a difference of degree than kind – a fleeting, personal thing rather than something that happens again and again, containing a message for all the world.

Things are even more different for the enquirer who is not a believer but is open to persuasion. Experiences which believers see as involving a divine presence will obviously carry no immediate conviction for non-believers because they are twice removed from them. But it would be very irrational for non-believers simply to dismiss this last class of evidence as a fiction, because there is good evidence to show that honest, reliable, sane, educated people from St Paul down to our own time have these experiences; they do indeed fit logically into the believer's world-view, and they would add weight to the case for theism if that case were already strong – provided we don't find grounds for preferring a naturalistic explanation of those experiences. And we have already seen why Christians find the most influential, naturalistic arguments very unsatisfactory indeed, failing to explain the rise and persistence of religion. That being so, greater weight attaches to the theistic explanation of these events, unless better naturalistic explanations can be produced. In the meantime, says the believer, these religious experiences point more towards God as their probable cause than anywhere else, possessing important objective status as proven facts in the experience of many people, and above all giving believers an immediate, felt sense that God is indeed utterly real, transforming their lives through Christ and the Holy Spirit into greater goodness and holiness. So we find the Christian's appeal to objective facts blending smoothly into the inner, subjective conviction that God truly exists and can be directly experienced in Christ and the Holy Spirit, the latter being safeguarded against self-deception by the public quality of the objective arguments.

This brings us to the end of the set of rational arguments given by Christians to justify their faith in a God in preference to rival philosophies. Believers are convinced that their arguments are stronger than their opponents. Whether they are correct will depend on the counter-arguments put forward by those who think there is no God, or who think that there is not enough grounding to make faith a rational position. Before we turn to this sceptical side of the debate, there are however two further steps that need to be taken. These are the Christian claim to possess the most satisfactory world-view, and a concluding summary of the case for the believer.

The Christian world-view

The Christian case is more than just a series of individual arguments. It is also a blending of these into a total view of reality which believers say is more factual and rational than its rivals. From a Christian point of view secularist world-views of all kinds like materialistic humanism or Marxism (considered as a total philosophy and not just as a theory about society) are furthest from the truth. World-views teaching that there is a spiritual basis to reality are judged by Christians to be much sounder in that respect than any form of secularism, with the God-believing religions placed nearer the truth than the non-theistic faiths. Though Christians nowadays are mostly too polite to say so, the logic of their own faith means quite definitely that they would rank Judaism and Islam (in that order) as coming next closest to Christianity, which they naturally think contains the fullest truth of all religions. But while this is what the historic mainline of Christianity *believes*, we have now seen that its thinkers also say that the superior truth of their faith can be shown by rational means as well, culminating in the total Christian world-view that was mentioned at the start of this paragraph.

Without a grasp of this total view we cannot therefore fully appreciate the meaning and alleged justification of Christianity. For Christians its superior truth lies essentially in two things: firstly the knowledge (as Christians see it) that God indeed exists and is perfect, almighty love, and secondly the reality of Christ as God's fullest revelation of himself, sealed and confirmed by the Holy Spirit. It is because of the first of these two points that Christians are logically obliged to rank the God-believing faiths above other religions and especially above humanism, materialism and Marxism, while the second point is the reason why they rank the Christian world-view above Judaism and Islam so far as fullness of truth is concerned.

The basic point is of course that the foundation of all things is God, an infinite, self-sufficient, personal being whose perfect love, goodness and almighty power are the driving force behind all else. He is the ultimate reality, the bedrock upon which all else stands secure, the source and goal of all things and of rational beings above all, as St Thomas Aquinas once said. As such he alone gives us the ultimate explanation of the cosmos. His loving nature expresses itself as a ceaseless well of creative energy bringing the whole of creation into being, which gives us the reason why there is a universe. But love's intention is that love should multiply and bring joy when it is both received and given, so God creates a universe which contains in it from the beginning the seeds of life, intelligence, freedom and thus the basis for love as well. It cannot be sufficiently emphasized how essential an insistence on freedom is to any rational case for God, because love can only be real amidst freedom, and in no other way can believers handle the problem of evil, than by arguing that a world made for love must be a world where there is freedom, and thus where some people will use their freedom in evil ways.

The result of God's creative intention is the world being discovered by biology and physics and all the other sciences, which helps us understand the remark Einstein is said to have made, that when he did the mathematics of modern physics he could hear God think.

Christianity thus teaches that ours is in fact a moral, rational and spiritual universe because it has been designed as the arena for intelligent, moral and ultimately spiritual life. Thus the open-minded study of nature points us onward from nature to its spiritual foundations, precisely as many scientists are now saying. But we all also know from experience that moral and spiritual qualities do not come about instantly. They are the result of a process of growth containing both mistakes and successes. They achieve depth and strength through hardship. As the English poet Jon Stallworthy once wrote, 'They walk most tall who learn to walk beneath a weight.' Philosopher of religion John Hick in his book *Evil and the God of Love* has helped Christians to understand how this explains the existence of natural evil – all those hardships like fire, disease and earthquakes which result from nature and not from human action. These things, says Hick, give us a God-given context in which moral struggle is possible, where things like fear and cowardice and cruelty are possible but are also capable of being overcome. A painless paradise for beings like ourselves would yield no moral growth, no possibility of advancing into the gift-like world of spiritual experience where compassion and creativity become realities.

Eventually, then, the creative process of the universe which God set in motion leads to the formation of our planet and its mantle of life. Eventually that mantle of life gives birth to our own species. Set in a world of pain as well as happiness, of things both clear to us and mysterious, our species finds that it has to make choices and take responsibility for them, so developing into a moral level of existence, and at the same time also learn the secrets of the world around it, so developing into intelligence. That is the knowledge of good and evil spoken of in the biblical story of creation. But any finite, fallible being who is free to make choices will sometimes choose selfish or harmful actions. This brings moral evil into the world, as we saw above, just as the generous and loving choices bring goodness into the world. The results of both are all around us every day.

As part of the same, magnificent adventure of human formation, the very mind that puzzles about the coming and going of the seasons, or of day and night, or life and death, puzzles also about where these things come from, dimly sensing the unseen presence of one who made it all happen. And the same conscience that slowly forms out of the growing experience of our human power to produce good and evil, also slowly and haltingly feels its way towards a sense that there is a moral power greater than our own. We know from the psychology of learning that the familiar acts as a model for the unknown, so it is perfectly natural that the human mind all over the planet should experience the rise of a religious sense. And what could be more likely than the god-concept which social scientists themselves tell us is a cultural universal? Feuerbach was right to say that we use the ideally human as the model for the god-concepts we unconsciously create and project into the heavens, says the Christian. But he was quite wrong, and spiritually very shallow, not to see that this is precisely what we should expect in a universe made by a God who wants there to be a multiplication of love and its joys, and who therefore wants the intelligent, moral creatures he has brought forth on this planet to find their own way to love of one another and the world around them and a loving knowledge of their divine source.

Believing as they do that the fullness of God's being is expressed above all by his everlasting love, and knowing from experience that even human love tries to help the needy, Christians argue that the next stage in their unfolding world-view also makes perfect sense. This is God's helping hand in history. Just as wise, loving parents know that they must allow their children scope to develop self-reliance while also actively helping them when the need arises, so God, as the perfect parent, sometimes gives humanity the help it needs, responding to the searching, spiritually awakening human mind with the revelations and miracles told of in the scriptures. This of course explains why we have people like Moses, Isaiah and Jeremiah, or events like the Exodus of the Hebrew slaves from Egypt, and why a great literature about these things and even more about the helping hand of God arose among the Jews. I refer of course to the Jewish scriptures, which Christians call the Old Testament.

The mainstream of Christianity believes that the moral and spirit-ual predicament of humanity was serious enough to need a final, climactic act of God's saving love. This took the form of his personal entry in history in the life of Christ at a time when there would be enough human moral and spiritual strength amidst the evils and sufferings of life, and enough education amidst the ignorance and superstition, to make it possible for Christ's loving example, offered as a free gift, both to win the equally free response of undying loyalty to him, and historical records strong enough as evidence to carry the truth of God's incarnation into the world in the form of the Gospels and other New Testament writings. As the climax within this climactic event, God's power, the same power which flowed miracu-lously from Jesus' hands during his lifetime, raised Jesus from the tomb to which his enemies had consigned him in order to give humanity due assurance that God is indeed as real, as active, as loving and as victorious as Jesus said he was. And with the deeply moving example of Christ's love, the power of the Holy Spirit and the channelling of both through the life of the church and its worship as sources of inspiration, people who come into the circle of Christian influence naturally experience their own transformation into better people. Some of them, now and then, even find their lives inspired to very great heights of saintliness as they try to follow the path of their Lord and Master.

The selfsame helping hand of God also explains the other miracles which believers report. As mere humans we cannot pretend to know God's mind on equal terms, and must accept, says the believer, that God will know best what to do when we find ourselves in some desperate predicament. If his infinite wisdom shows that the cause of love and truth are best served by intervening in response to the call for his help, then he intervenes. That is why miracles cannot be predicted, and why even the most devout of believers knows that his or her prayers for a miracle may not be met. It all makes perfect sense when seen at a spiritual level, says the Christian believer.

All of this means that the world is not just the theatre of natural forces studied by science. It is not just matter and energy shaping and reshaping themselves into the endless variety of things we observe around and in us. In addition it is a world of moral, rational and spiritual reality permeating physical things and becoming evident to the awakening moral and spiritual potential of the human mind. To that inner eye, which opens when a pure and generous faith combines with a clear and honest ability to reason, the world of time and space appears unmistakably, says the believer, as God's world, as a world in which his everlasting and awe-inspiring love are everywhere present, even in what the ordinary human eye regards as the darkest corners of evil. Small wonder, then, the believer goes on to say, that we find God-conscious people reporting religious experiences quite often, revealing vividly to them for a brief time the glorious reality of God – a God who is either found and accepted as a gift or mistaken as a delusion.

Summary and conclusion

As we have seen in this chapter, the modern Christian case for faith in God begins with the conviction that Jesus Christ himself is the primary window, as it were, through which we may see God with the eye of both faith and reason. Jesus taught by word and deed that God was an eternally and perfectly loving being, of whom he himself was most intimately aware, and we have very reliable historical records in the New Testament containing those teachings. We also have significant documentary material from the same source claiming that Jesus was raised from the dead by the power of God, which – if true – would mean that Jesus' teachings were not merely his own, fallible, human thoughts about God, but had been given a dramatic seal of approval by God himself. Viewed with an open mind, this documentary material cannot be ignored or belittled, because it meets the historian's norms for sound evidence. It must thus be faced fairly and squarely, and the question must then be asked which is more probable – that the Jesus tradition is in fact a valid indication of the existence of a loving God, as it claims to be, or that it is not. Christians hold that the facts about Jesus point rational enquirers more towards God as the cause of those facts than towards any other explanation, but concede that other explanations are theoretically possible. This makes us ask why we should prefer the former.

The way to settle this key question is to examine and test the other, independent grounds for theism. If these give us significant, rational grounds for belief in the existence of God, that would make it reasonable to favour Christianity's claims about Jesus Christ as himself giving evidence of God, especially if the sceptical case has its own, internal problems. As we have seen, believers draw on philosophy, physics, biology, anthropology, morality and the history of religion to mount a substantial, impressive argument in support of their world-view, with evidence about miracles and religious experiences of a divine presence providing what they regard as strong confirmation for an already powerful case. Blending all of these points into a coherent whole, Christianity is thus able to offer humanity a world-view which believers find more comprehensive, more factually sound and more logical than any of its rivals. In particular it far surpasses the various secularist philosophies because of what believers see as their grossly defective accounts of religion itself and their blindness concerning God. But Christians also find it sounder than the other religions, especially the ones which have no concept of God. In view of the evidence from biology, physics and elsewhere, this absence of a sense of God's reality inevitably strikes Christians as a fatal gap in those religions, even though there is much that is otherwise morally and spiritually superb in them. And finally, Christians argue that the facts of history, contained in authentic sources preserved in the New Testament, mean that no religion – even one that believes in God – can be fully in touch with the truth if it does not recognize in Jesus of Nazareth the very presence of God himself.

As will already be clear, the debate about God being explored in this book in fact involves a careful weighing up of the merits of rival world-views – one centred upon belief in a loving, infinite God who, according to Christians, became incarnate in Jesus of Nazareth; the others containing only the natural universe or some other kind of spiritual power but not the God whom Jesus is said to embody – each of them using a complex set of arguments. As we turn now to hear the sceptic's side of this enormously important debate, let us remember that the impressive-sounding case by the Christian believer must be measured against a rival's case we have not yet heard, a rival whom we must listen to as fully and fairly as we have listened to the believer.

What would that sceptical rival have to do to win the debate? It seems that two things would have to be achieved. Firstly, the believer's case must be refuted ar at least significantly weakened. And secondly, we must be shown by facts and logical arguments that a non-Christian world-view does a better job of explaining the whole of our experience than the Christian one. To make it irrational to believe, Christianity's critics must show that Christian theism is clearly less probable than its rivals, all things considered. Can they do this? Let us turn to their side of the debate in order to find out.

3

The Case against the Believer

Over four hundred years ago the Protestant leader John Calvin made Geneva his base. He set up a God-centred government there which became the springboard for the Calvinist movement that spread to many Western countries. Its religious influence has been great, especially in places like Scotland, the USA, the Netherlands – and South Africa, where Dutch Calvinists were the first European conquerors to settle. But Calvinism, like Islam, is not just a religious movement. It is an attempt to re-organize the whole of life, and this carries its impact into politics, social life and the economy. The famous social thinker Max Weber even developed an extremely important theory that Calvinism supplied the outlook which made modern capitalism possible. If that theory is even partly correct, then Calvinism has been one of the most influential forces shaping much of the modern Western world.

Unlike Rio de Janeiro with its famous statue of Christ, Geneva has no massive monument to Calvin on the hills overlooking the city, though it has no shortage of banks. But Calvin's church still stands in the old part of the city, and his chair can be seen there to this day. Surprising small and appropriately austere, it triggers thoughts about the power of his type of burning conviction that God truly exists and must rule all aspects of life.

But there is also a newer, and very different, symbolic reality in Geneva, the many international agencies with headquarters there. They show us another kind of experiment, an attempt through human effort to bring harmony and co-operation into world affairs. And of these agencies one in particular is significant for this book. This is the European Centre for Nuclear Research – known mostly by its French acronym CERN – at the edge of the city beyond the airport. Here is assembled perhaps the greatest concentration of scientific expertise in history from many nations and world-views, with the common purpose of extending the frontiers of knowledge concerning the fundamental nature of matter and energy for peaceful purposes. The buildings, experiment halls, equipment and sheer state-of-the-art scale of CERN are quite stunning for the layperson, and few non-physicists would follow the technicalities of this vast, multinational enterprise.

But one key detail at CERN is unmistakable. As is the case in so many institutions of the modern world, it is a *secular* project. This does not mean that the scientists who work there are all atheists or agnostics, for they are not. Nor does it mean that the Centre has a bias against believers. What it does mean is that personal religious beliefs are irrelevant to the task in hand in a way that is quite impossible in any church. And the successes already achieved struck me, as I reflected on the place, as evidence of a successful human reality very unlike that announced in cathedral and church – a successful human venture where faith in a God plays no official part at all. Where such faith exists it does so as a private matter for the individuals concerned. Nothing could be further from Calvin's view of the proper place of God. This makes me ask what happens at places like CERN to his burning sense that God is sovereign everywhere? What happens to any form of Christianity there – and in the thousands of other places on earth where faith in God is either irrelevant or even seen as wholly deluded? If we are to answer that question we must look with great care and fairness at the view of those who see things this way. That is the aim of this chapter.

Though believers sometimes do not know this fact and occasionally even deny that it possible, the world has vast numbers of decent, thoughtful people who see belief in God as a delusion, as a remnant from humanity's mental and spiritual childhood. Most Buddhists, Taoists and Confucians, many Hindus, virtually all Marxists and millions of secular-minded Westerners hold this view, living meaningful and moral lives without experiencing any need for the concept of God. It is thus a serious mistake to think of theism as normal for all of humanity, and of atheism and agnosticism (the view that we

79

...ow whether there is a God or not) as marginal. This is
...ly how things look to many people in the Western and
... worlds. But globally it is not so. God-believing people
ce...inly seem to be a majority world-wide, but there is a very sizable,
non-theistic community as well.

When we turn to the arguments against belief in God it is vital that
we keep in mind this global, non-theistic community, remembering
especially that it contains two main sections: an age-old group of
religious people who report that faith can do perfectly well without
the concept of God, and secondly the various *secular* world-views,
especially humanism and Marxism, which follow no religious path
at all. These have shown great numerical growth over the past century
or two, but are not products of the modern world alone. They have
roots in the thought of ancient Greece and Rome, well before the
time of Christ, going back to people like Democritus and Epicurus
whose materialist theories are an important ancestor of modern
science.

As we saw in chapter 1, previous accounts of the debate about
God have generally made the mistake of seeing it merely as a debate
between believers and secularists, leaving out the hundreds of millions
of *religious* people who are just as sceptical about Christian theism
as any humanist or Marxist. We will avoid that error and review a
much fuller spectrum of arguments against the Christian believer.
We must picture in our imaginations a group of thoughtful Christians
on one side – whom we have already heard – and a mixed group
of thoughtful non-Christians on the other, some of them secular
humanists in the Western countries, some of them Marxists, but
some of them Buddhists, Hindus or Taoists. There is even a small
but significant group of Christians for whom belief in God has
become irrelevant and spiritually harmful, Don Cupitt at Cambridge
being the best known.

It is their side of the debate we must now hear. Obviously they
differ about many things. But they agree about a central point: it is
a mistake, they say, to suppose that the God spoken of by believers
really exists, a subtle and hard-to-detect mistake which has every
appearance of being utterly realistic, but nonetheless a mistake. And
as we shall see below, this sceptical group will call in support of their

case two important but unexpected groups of witnesses. They will call on Jews, Muslims and other theists from outside Christianity to add important further evidence for the rejection of Christian theism. And they will call on people from the women's movement who claim to have exposed the traditional Christian concept of God as sexist and oppressive, and therefore as a masculinist misrepresentation of the truth. Thus we can see that the full debate about the orthodox Christian view of God pits the world's Christians – numbering about one third of humanity – against the rest of the human race and even against some Christians in the women's movement and elsewhere. That in itself is food for thought.

The case against the Christian theist therefore opens with an important reminder to us all that most members of our species believe Christians are wrong about God. On the other hand, the world's Muslims, Jews and other monotheists in the Indian and African religions (and elsewhere) certainly agree with Christians that there is a God. What they reject is the specifically Christian idea that God's loving desire to save the world is chiefly and uniquely expressed in Jesus Christ and the New Testament scriptures, so that Jesus is the only saviour. Against this Christian view of God, rejected by about two-thirds of humanity, the most radical opposition is however from the various secularist world-views. These reject any idea that there is an independent spiritual reality of some kind or other, whether it be a single God or an all-embracing spiritual force surpassing but also permeating the physical universe. In short, secularists regard all religions as mistaken, however noble their moral teachings may be. In most regions where Christianity is the main religion, the debate about God is first and foremost a debate between Christians and these secularists who offer the most radical challenge to Christian theism, so we will concentrate on that form of the debate. But in doing so we will also give very careful attention to the way other kinds of believer enter the debate against Christianity as well, including other monotheists.

In response to the rich set of arguments given by Christian believers in God, but using exactly the same rules of reasoning, these secularist sceptics say firstly that their own experience and world-view provide a very convincing basis for rejecting the idea that there is a God;

...that the set of arguments based on philosophy, science, ...religion and morality is unsound and unable to show that ...s a God, and thirdly that even the genuine facts concerning Jesu... of Nazareth and the believers' sense of inner, personal assurance about their God fit very well into their secular world-view. Crucially, they claim that their world-view even makes better sense of the facts of religion as a whole than Christianity or any other God-orientated religion. Let us turn now to the details of these bold and potentially far-reaching contentions.

Experiencing the absence of a God

Believers are often puzzled that anybody could doubt or reject the idea that there is a God. Yet there are hundreds of millions who do because they find nothing in their experience that gives the least indication of God. We cannot hope to understand their views until we grasp this key point. To show how easy it is to mistake it, we need do no more than remember that most people define an atheist or non-theist as somebody who 'denies' the existence of God. This definition biases the whole question in favour of the believer by assuming that God exists, and then implies – very unfairly – that those who say there is no God are turning their backs on or 'denying' reality. If we begin our tour of the case against Christian faith in God by repeating this error we would already be begging the question against the sceptics. Clearly that will not do. Instead, therefore, we will look at things through their eyes, which means grasping that their experience reveals nothing in the least godlike.

The point was excellently put by William Hamilton a few decades ago when thinkers like him were announcing that 'God is dead'. 'We are not talking', he said, 'about the absence of the experience of God, but about the experience of the absence of God.' This is a matter of looking long and hard at the way we experience life and finding that there simply is no sign of God anywhere. More positively, it is a matter of finding that life has meaning, purpose and value without the slightest reference to a deity. This doesn't prove that there is no deity, but it certainly leaves those who have this experience of the absence of God without any personal basis for thinking that there might be one. Instead, belief in God sounds to them like a day dream, a fantasy, or an outdated way of thinking, and they are left with no choice but to reject as quite wrong the allegation reportedly made by the seventeenth-century French mathematician and religious thinker Blaise Pascal, to the effect that there is a 'God-shaped vacuum' in everybody. If he had in mind the Christian concept of God, then it simply isn't true in the experience of many people.

As I said above, until we grasp the reality of this experience of having no need for the God-idea, we cannot do justice to the argument against the believer. That is perhaps the chief problem besetting Brian Hebblethwaite's defence of theism in his lively and stimulating book *The Ocean of Truth*. He tries to counter the views of his fellow Cambridge religious thinker Don Cupitt, who has written plenty about the discovery, as he and others see it, that there is no God, and makes some telling points. But the book (and all others like it that I have seen) seems to me to miss what is often most compelling in the life of secularists and other non-theists, and that is the day-by-day experience of the absence of a God. So we must make our way through the sceptics' territory by understanding that we will be hearing from people who sincerely find that God-talk is just that – a lot of nice-sounding talk but no more. Most of them are too polite to say so, but theism reminds them of the story of the emperor's new clothes, which were also all talk and no substance. As they see things, atheists and non-theists are not 'denying' something very real; they are simply being true to their own experience and challenging what they see as delusions clouding the minds of believers.

A long and rich secular heritage

As I pointed out briefly above, over the past few centuries the number of these people has grown significantly in the West, though it is probably still a minority except perhaps in some universities. But this must not delude us into thinking that life without the concept of God is something recent. Quite the contrary is true, for modern secularism has its roots in the ancient world before and independently of the rise of Christianity. Ancient Greek and Roman civilization and the even older civilizations of China, ancient India, Mesopotamia and

Egypt, with their own immense accomplishments, were the work of men and women who found fulfilment and meaning without faith in a God as understood by Christians. The first experiments with democratic government, the invention of writing, the agricultural revolution, the birth of science and philosophy and of great art and architecture, all these great achievements and many more took place outside and sometimes before the rise of monotheistic faith. Some of them, like the science of the ancient Mediterranean world, even went into decline after the rise of the church. So when we visit Rome today and see the many symbols of Christian eminence, we should also remember that a great civilization reigned there long before Christian belief in God took over. Certainly it had its bad side (just like the church), but it also had many glories – glories of human achievement unaided by what Christians think of as the grace of God.

When the church started losing power in Europe from about 1500 onwards that ancient human heritage began to regain vitality. Its modern growth has run parallel with things like the rebirth of science, the rise of secularization (the trend whereby religious control over society's main institutions is replaced by non-religious structures) and of modern democratic government. While the majority of Westerners has continued to be Christian (though here too there has been extensive liberalizing of old beliefs in many circles), others found that they could prosper without church or biblical guidance and even without faith in God. The result has been the gradual forming of a new kind of Western world-view, a secularist world-view which believes that the only reality is the physical universe. Secularists think this new world-view is much more plausible than anything the churches can produce. In order to compare its merits with the Christian world-view which we discussed in the previous chapter, let us turn now to the way secularists see things. That will give us the full platform on which their response to the case for Christian theism stands.

A naturalistic world-view

The famous scientific thinker Carl Sagan began his television series *Cosmos* a few years ago with a vivid summary of the belief that

84

nature is the only reality. 'Cosmos', he said, 'is all there e
all there ever will be, and you and I are made of star-stuf
words, secularists regard the universe itself as the ultima
rejecting the religious notion that there is a higher, inde, ...uent,
spiritual reality as well. Whether the universe had a beginning or is
eternal is for them an unsettled question at present, but if it can be
settled, science and science-based philosophy will do so, not religion,
especially God-orientated religion. Least of all, they say, will it be
settled by biblically fundamentalist religion. Till then we must just
accept that our knowledge is still too limited to answer that question.

The next point is that the universe is what it is on its own. Nothing
else and nobody else (for example a God) has made it be what it is.
Secularists therefore believe in what is sometimes called a 'brute-fact
universe'. This means that we shouldn't ask where it came from or
who made it, because the universe itself simply exists as a brute fact
with nothing more basic to rest upon, just as God is seen as a sort of
'brute-fact God' by believers. Similarly, its marvellous, life-giving
character is also seen as a fact of nature. That this seems incredibly
unlikely may be so at the present stage of our path to fuller knowledge,
and must be left for future scientific discoveries and philosophic
breakthroughs to explain. Long ago it also seemed incredible that
rain fell from the skies without a god causing it, and everybody
'knew' that the great mother goddess caused the earth to bring forth
new life each spring. But now we know better and would rightly
react in utter disbelief if the weather announcer on TV solemnly told
us that one of the gods was causing the latest cold front or heat wave.
We now know better than to turn to religion when our scientific
knowledge reaches its limits at any given time, says the sceptic.
Taking refuge in the God-concept when human resources are, for
the moment, fruitless is even sometimes seen as an unworthily juvenile
reaction. Instead, say these people, we must find the realism and
courage to accept that there is nobody out there to help us out of
trouble, and nobody to solve our scientific puzzles other than
ourselves.

Thus the cosmos is seen as sufficient to itself. Its orderly processes
and the laws which describe them are facts of nature, not the gifts of
a God. Within the great cosmic process since the big bang a stage

came when the fiery matter near certain stars cooled enough to form systems of planets, one of them our own solar system in the gravitional field of the lesser star we know as our sun. And because of its position, size, composition and daily rotation, one of the planets in our system – planet earth – would, as Arthur Clarke so memorably wrote, be the sun's favourite child lying mid-way between fire and ice, positioned for life. In the mind-boggling vastness of just our own galaxy there is nothing in the least surprising that somewhere there would be such a planet, a planet possessing the chemical raw materials and energy sources needed for life.

By means of natural forces which we do not now fully understand but will one day solve and imitate, the secularists continue, those raw materials, under the action of natural forms of energy like the sun and lightning acting on a planet that steadily cooled and stabilized, underwent the changes that led to the first forms of life. There is no need to seek here the hand of heavenly beings, say the secularists. Natural forces acting on natural substances over vast periods of time are enough, because science has already achieved spectacular success by refusing to use the God-concept to 'explain' nature's puzzles. Instead it has chosen the long, slow and difficult but marvellously successful path of naturalistic enquiry. Had this policy proved barren or only partly fertile there might be reason to change it. But, add the sceptics, it has not proved to be like that at all, so there is no reason to drop our electron microscopes and reach for our Bibles.

Thus Begun, the process of natural evolution continues. The amazing potential of the cosmos to produce life spontaneously in ever more varied and complex forms was realized on our planet and perhaps on many others, doing so in conditions that naturally included destructive as well as protective agencies: fire, hurricane, ultra-violet radiation and drought as well as sunshine, food and rain. What else would we expect to find in a cosmos that began with the big bang? Amidst those conditions mobile kinds of life eventually emerged, creatures with limbs, fins or wings. The power of movement carried the danger of straying into harmful or fatal environments unless there was equipment that could compensate for that danger. If we look at the mobile species that have survived we can see what that equipment was: protective skins or coats, alert senses and the like. But in due course the process gave rise to mobile living things with a hugely important set of new, compensatory characteristics – the ability to feel pain and pleasure (known as sentience) and the ability to remember those sensations and avoid the former but seek the latter.

Coupled with the transition by some mammalian species to bipedalism, which means walking upright on two legs, so freeing the forelimbs for possible tool-use, we have here the basis for intelligent, moral life and the creation of culture, including religion. When brains complex enough for sentience, memory and consciousness evolved, they also achieved the powers of learning and of modifying behaviour in the light of experience, and that is at least part of the meaning of intelligence. So too they created the foundations of moral life, because morality rests, among other things, on the ability to judge and sort our actions into opposing categories – those that we approve of (the 'good' ones) and those we dislike. On a planet affected by both helpful and harmful conditions as ours is, a mobile being which can stray from its safe, native habitat is made endlessly more resilient by this ability to judge between beneficial and harmful things.

Sentience makes the brain capable of those acts of judgment and sorting. Along with memory it is the bridge to a moral sense, because remembered experiences of pain and happiness enable a being equipped for sentience to begin to recognize that there is on the one hand a class of things that must be resisted and even forbidden, and on the other a class of things to be praised and encouraged. Thus nature reaches the level of the early human, unaided by gods or anything else outside itself, according to this view. And humans, with their characteristic abilities of learning something from their experience, of desiring new ways of doing things, of adjusting their behaviour accordingly and so constructing new patterns of living in virtually every kind of environment on this planet, thereby became cultural rather than biological beings. Decision rather than instinct or genetic coding became the mainspring of their existence, and that is a large part of what we mean when we say humanity has free will, which is precisely the ability to recognize and choose between alternative actions and then enact those decisions in ways that change our conditions.) Compare human life with any other kind and the difference in this respect is obvious: we alone of all species have almost totally changed the conditions in which we live, whereas even the large-brained dolphins and the other primates have remained in their environmental cradles. Culture is the name we give to all the things humanity has created and passed on by means other than the biological in the course of this long process of changing nature by means of nature's own gifts of memory, sentience, hands with opposable thumbs and above all conscious creativity.

The learning process in humans involves another vital aspect. When we encounter something very strange, how do we find out what it is? Nowadays we ask others, but how did they find out? How is something which nobody knows made intelligible, like earlier generations trying to understand eclipses of the sun or moon? The evidence shows that the unknown object will defy comprehension unless it can be associated with something we already know, for example through resemblance or contrast. Thus the first settlers in a country like Australia called koalas 'bears', and the early Afrikaners in Southern Africa named the giraffe the 'camel-horse'. And when they trekked into the interior they named the first north-flowing stream the Nile because they had heard that the Nile flows northward, uniquely among African rivers, or so they thought. Henri Frankfort's book *Before Philosophy* tells us that the ancient Egyptians (using the identical device of defining the strange in terms of the familiar) even called rain 'Nile-in-the-sky'.

From this it follows that in general humanity has tried to fathom the many strange things it has encountered on its path from near-total ignorance to rising knowledge by means of anything suitable and already familiar. But what is more familiar to humanity than itself? It is not in the least surprising, then, that the belief formed that out there beyond our ken there are unseen personal beings modelled on the human, beings who make things happen.) Our ancestors naturally and inevitably learnt that there is a principle of cause-and-effect (for example by remembering similar pains after similar accidents). That made it possible to wonder what caused things like day and night, the seasons, fertility or natural disasters, for which there are no obvious, visible causes. Humanity's natural device when faced with such puzzles – and let us notice that often these are life-affecting puzzles, not just mental games – is the unconscious belief that there must be *somebody* out there making these things happen. The human model provides a first way of trying to work out why these things happen. And in view of the importance of the mysteries being encountered, what would be more natural than the rise of a belief that the unseen beings out there must be very much mightier than any of us, and therefore worthy of the utmost respect?

In this way the secularists find no great difficulty in explaining why people have developed a world-wide belief in gods and other personal spirits, unconsciously inventing the very deities they worship. The supernatural turns out, on this view, to be no more than nature in disguise. Of course the experienced powers associated with these supposed deities are all too real. Secularists know that, but regard those powers as what we today would call the forces of nature.

It is here that the insights of the women's movement are especially valuable. While there are many feminists who remain in the Christian churches, everybody in the movement for women's liberation agrees that there is a very serious sexist or masculinist bias in most religions, and certainly in Christianity. This shows itself in the way power, status and positions in the churches are overwhelmingly in the hands of men (a situation known as patriarchy); but its most insidious facet is the way male symbols dominate the minds of Christians, unconsciously but forcefully fostering a male-centred world-view which has done terrible harm and injustice to the equal spiritual rights of women – a situation known as androcentrism – making the male the symbolic model for the important things in life. Christian feminists challenge outright the belief that these male-centred notions – that God is our Father, our King or our Shepherd, that priests must be male and that husbands must rule the family – are God-given revelations of truth. Instead, they are seen as merely masculinist misinterpretations of divine reality created unconsciously by power-wielding men in the distant past and passed off by their more recent male heirs as sacred truths in order to entrench their own power and privileges.

This view fits perfectly into a naturalistic world-view, say the sceptics, except that secularists obviously deny that God-talk is in any sense about a genuine divine reality. The point being made here is that the official concept of God in virtually all theistic religion and certainly in Christianity obviously has a male form. Secularists welcome the data produced by the women's movement about this fact, and then point out that this masculinist bias is just what we would expect when the mental processes described above take place in male-dominated cultures. The familiar model which subtly guides society's sense of the divine will then be male-orientated because males are in charge of everything, even of thought. So there is no need at all to think that the God-concept must come from God when liberated Christian women know better than that. They know it is not even a human creation. It is, we are told, merely a masculinist creation which got where it is by suppressing women for countless centuries.

Thus a naturalistic world-view claims to provide a much better explanation of theism than theism itself, with its bias in favour of the male. Turning now to to other points we must ask why something like love should be so central in many religions unless it comes from beyond humanity and nature? Is love not contrary to nature's way, which is the alleged instinct for self-preservation and predation? Drawing on the sociobiology of scientists like E.O. Wilson and other naturalistic scientists, secularists also have an answer for this question. Species like the social insects whose genetic make-up is coded for altruistic behaviour (where individuals risk and even sacrifice their lives for others of their kind) will have a definite advantage over rivals who lack that coding. Exactly the same holds for other species, including humans, whose altruistic behaviour is mostly directed at close relatives and therefore enhances the survival of those whose genetic make-up is closest to that of the altruist.) What we call love and think of as a moral and spiritual quality turns out to have definite survival value – not for the individual who gives up its life, of course, but for its kind. That in turn increases the chances of survival for future individuals, so there is no mystery about human cultures making a big thing about love and selflessness, and using religious beliefs to entrench them. What could be more beneficial (even in a purely physical sense) in the long run than a widespread belief that there are spiritual beings more powerful than we ourselves who want us to behave in loving ways? Any group with that notion firmly implanted in its thinking will have a definite advantage over others. So nature once again proves sufficient, say the secularists, to explain things, making the God-hypothesis irrelevant. The scientist Laplace is said to have told Napoleon that he had no need of that God-hypothesis in his science. Now we find secularists saying they also have no need of it in order to explain religion. Nature and the unaided powers of humankind are said to be sufficient.

The same holds for belief in one, supreme deity. Secularists point out that monotheism became prominent at a time when human society had become familiar with roles like kingship and other forms of individual prominence. The natural effect would be to foster notions that there is also a leader or king among the gods. And if a culture happened to depend very much on a single reality like agriculture or warfare to survive, then it would be very natural for it to treat the goddess of the earth or the god of war as specially important, and to close ranks against the gods of its neighbours. In that way a tendency towards monotheism would be encouraged by cultural forces, and if the people concerned survived (as some obviously did, or we wouldn't be here), then that itself would push the process along even further because devotion to that one deity had been fruitful. As we all know, few things attract us humans more than fruitful policies; sentient experience has shown that those who set up camp near an oasis survive; those who think the desert is better do not.

There is no need to take the story further than this. It is already enough to show us the scope and persuasiveness of the world-view that has formed in secularist circles. People in those circles hold that it is able to cover every facet of our experience, including morality and religion, without leaving anything unexplained. Above all, they assert that it shows that the concept of God is redundant as a way of accounting for things. Later in this chapter we will have to return to aspects of this naturalistic world-view in order to see how sceptics explain the facts about Jesus of Nazareth. But for the meantime we have enough to allow us to appreciate the next part of the sceptics' case, namely their rejection of the set of objective arguments given by Christians, which are supposed to show that there are convincing, independent grounds for believing that there is a God.

What really is the ultimate reality?

While all theists agree with Christians that God is the ultimate reality and thus the ultimate explanation for the existence of anything at all, there are rival arguments which undercut the believer's convictions at this point too. Buddhists, Taoists and all others whose religion sees no need for the God-concept say that their religious experience reveals that an all-inclusive spiritual reality is in fact ultimate, not a personal deity. We shall see more of this argument later in the chapter, but the key point must be grasped now. If there really is a self-sufficient God who is the adequate ground of all else, then why do so many people experience something quite different, like Nirvana, Brahman or the Tao – none of which is a divine person – as the bedrock of reality when they become expert at concentrating their minds on spiritual matters? This does not prove that there is no God but it definitely places a question mark over the arguments of believers who think that theirs is the only viable candidate for giving us an ultimate explanation for reality as a whole. It is even sometimes argued that a personal God *cannot* be ultimate because to be personal is something specific and thus limits God to that specific characteristic. In that case God would allegedly not be infinite and all-encompassing, and thus not ultimate.

So we find the religious world divided about what really is ultimate, with theists so far being unable to persuade other kinds of believer that they are correct. An excellent discussion of this important state of affairs is given by John B. Cobb Jr in his book *Beyond Dialogue: Towards a Mutual Transformation of Christianity and Buddhism*. Himself a Christian, Cobb describes very convincingly the sophisticated philosophical account of the ultimate given by Buddhists. He regards this sophistication as something Christians can learn from their Eastern co-religionists, which hardly inspires confidence in the notion that the traditional Christian concept of God is the best account of ultimate reality.

So far I have discussed only the clash of belief between theists and

non-theistic believers. But the world's non-Christian
especially Muslims and Jews, could also criticize th
concept of ultimate reality. By means of the philosophical
a simple reality has greater prior probability than anything ⟨ ...plex,
they could point out that Christianity's Trinitarian view of God
indicates a being who would be less simple than the deity of those
other monotheistic religions. That makes their view more probable,
other things being equal, than Christianity's view.

Secularists also reject theism on this issue, but for very different
reasons. One of them is the point that finite minds like ours are ill-
suited to settling ultimate questions and should thus not be dogmatic
about them. Confucius and after him Socrates can hardly be called
modern secularists but their reminder that it is knowledge and not
ignorance to acknowledge ignorance is a good indication of this
point. It is intended to discourage people from assuming that when
our ordinary stock of answers fails to meet some problem we must
conclude that God is the answer, but rather accept our limitations
for the time being and keep looking for naturalistic answers.

This reaction in effect questions the whole enterprise of believing
that humanity can reliably find an ultimate explanation for things.
To accept our limitations, says the sceptic, is not in the least mentally
demeaning or obscurantist, it is simply being realistic. Even so
resolute a believer as Blaise Pascal, the famous French mathematician
of the seventeenth century, admitted as much in his memorable work
Pensées (Thoughts), when he wrote that nothing is more agreeable
to reason than to know when it is out of its depth. He intended this
as an aid to faith in God but the point applies just as much in reverse.

There is a further, secularist objection to the believer, to the effect
that the universe itself is self-sufficient and eternal, possessing within
its infinity everything needed to explain the particular facts around
us. This implies a vastly bigger concept of the universe than the usual
one of the expanding system of matter/energy that commenced with
the big bang. It would involve a virtually infinite set of cosmic regions
within a sort of mega-cosmos, in which an utterly vast range of
conditions is realized. Since we humans are not all-knowing, this
possibility cannot be ruled out. Why should we assume that our
present notions about the universe are the final stage of discovery,

just because that seems to suit the theist? Sceptics remind us at this point that we would rightly reject the argument, made in the Middle Ages or earlier before modern scientific studies of the weather, that since nothing known to us can get vast amounts of water into the sky, there must be a god who causes rain. Increased knowledge refutes that view, which should caution us against premature notions about the limits of nature.

As for the kalam argument in favour of a divine creator, secular-ists can accept the notion of a beginning to the universe but reject the further idea that a spontaneous universe is necessarily improbable. Ordinary experience certainly shows that things have causes, but we are not talking about ordinary things now, they say. We are talking about the whole universe, and we humans simply have no stock of experience about universes. That makes it illogical to treat the latter as we would all other things, like missing cats or landslides. And in any case, modern physics now reportedly has laboratory evidence at the sub-atomic level of spontaneous existence.

In sum, sceptics of various kinds believe they have shown that while God would indeed theoretically provide an ultimate explanation for reality if he exists, we have other answers to that problem which believers have not refuted. That weakens their case. Also, they remind us of our own mental limitations when we set off in search of an ultimate explanation for things, and warn us to be wary of claims to have found it. If this is the sort of question we humans really are capable of correctly answering, they ask, why do we keep producing conflicting answers to it? And lastly, the universe itself could in fact be the ultimate reality, or have come into being spontaneously. Nobody has proved that to be impossible.

Is modern physics really the believer's ally?

There are various books by believers explaining how – according to them – the latest physics backs the believer, but the argument really boils down to the neat expression given by Cambridge theologian Brian Hebblethwaite : the life-giving universe revealed by physics indicates the presence of an explicit *intention* behind it. So far as we know, only intelligent beings have intentions. If the best explanation of the the universe points us towards intention, then it also points us towards a massively powerful mind – in short, towards God.

What do sceptics say in response to this argument? Their first response is that the universe studied by physics is the same universe as the one studied by biologists and everybody else, so that the God-theory must be judged in relation to the full range of facts about the world, and not just the findings of physics. Thus the sceptics link their response at this point to the things they have to say about biology and God, which we will consider in the next section. But for the present we may note that the full reality revealed by the sciences and our own experience is that whoever (or whatever) caused the universe – assuming for argument's sake that it had a cause in the first place – did not merely intend that there should be order, life and intelligence in the universe, but also planned a universe where there is agony and disease, and – ironically – intelligent humans who experience the deepest anguish at the savagery that seems to be built into the system of animal life of which they are part, especially its relentless, predatory cruelties and the often ugly process of decomposition to which all of it is headed, and some of whose more thoughtful and moral members want to know how these evils fit into the picture of a perfect creator? Whoever intended all of this must have knowingly arranged things in the big bang where it all began so that this very reality with its many ugly, natural features would result, and not any of the others that were possible. Intention there may well be, but how, ask these people, can it possibly be the kind of infinitely loving intention required by Christians and other theists?

There are sceptics who scorn and ridicule believers for their seeming superficiality and convenient one-sidedness in ignoring or playing down this side of nature. Other sceptics see ridicule as unworthy of human thought, and react more with a sense of sadness that the impressive concept of God taught by religions like Christianity should be so impossible (so it seems) to reconcile with the facts; that the kind of God for whom so many people long with all their hearts should be so firmly ruled out of the question by the full range of scientific fact. Remembering Freud's theory of religion, they wonder whether he was not right after all when he said that reality is too disturbing for most of us to face, so that we unconsciously invent comforting delusions to let us cope, above all the delusion that somebody strong and father-like is out there in charge of things.)

So far the sceptical reaction to the 'physics-points-us-to-God' argument has conceded that the universe rests upon intention rather than upon blind forces of nature, and attacks the idea that this intention is perfectly good and loving. But should we concede even that much to the believer? Does the universe really indicate the likely presence of intention in the first place? It seemed to me that even this would have to be checked, and what better way could there be than to check it at the Mecca of particle physics, namely CERN?

So I made my way there, passing through Geneva and noting its symbolic richness for the debate about God because of the links with both Calvin and the more recent, human quest for a peaceful, co-operative world where disputes are settled rationally and not by the strong and the greedy copying the ways of the crocodile. With the help of one of the Directors of Research I was able to raise the question of intention with two scientists there who specialize in things relevant to my investigation. They were cosmologist Dr Andrei Linde (now at Stanford University in the USA) and particle-physics theorist Dr John Ellis. Here then were scientists at what is arguably the citadel of this kind of physics, whose computer screens and personal presence put them in direct touch with the most up-to-date particle physics in the world to provide the best possible data in response to my questions.

I met these two scientists separately, explained that I was working on a book about the God-question, asked for their views about cosmology and put the same key question to them both: did they agree that the universe being revealed by the latest physics indeed indicates the presence of intention? Is God indeed the most likely explanation for the incredible, life- and intelligence-giving characteristics of the cosmos? Both of them independently gave the same answer: the universe does *not* indicate to them as physicists the presence of intention. Dr Linde, whose comments included Eastern and Western religious thought, started by explaining that he had problems with the standard, big bang theory of the universe. Instead, he proposes what he calls a 'chaotic, self-reproducing inflationary universe'. In words printed at the start of his article in the September

1987 issue of *Physics Today*, his view is summarized as follows: 'It seems likely that the universe is an eternal, self-reproducing entity divided into many mini-universes . . .' (p. 61).

So far as the God-hypothesis is concerned, Dr Linde responded that there are many models of God, the most primitive in his view being the idea of a person with a will. And concerning the claim that our present picture of the cosmos indicates intention as its basic cause, he gave me leave to quote him as saying that 'at the moment we do not have enough arguments to say the universe is the result of intention'.

Dr Linde's statements were not meant as and must not be confused with a proof that there is no God. But even though he would not describe himself as an atheist and sees problems in the standard scientific approach which neglects consciousness (discussed in pp. 316-17 of his book *Particle Physics and Inflationary Cosmology*) his views definitely raise doubts about the believer's argument that the latest physics points us towards God as defined in this book. In fact, his words and the article mentioned above seem to me to mean very clearly that the latest physics makes the God-hypothesis, as usually understood, an unlikely and somewhat unsophisticated option so far as the latest particle physics-based cosmology is concerned.

My meeting with Dr John Ellis strengthened this impression. 'Not at all,' was his reaction to being asked whether the universe indicates a personal purpose. 'I don't see any evidence of intention.' He was obviously very well aware of the believer's attempt to harness modern physics to the wagon of faith, and considerately explained some differences between classical and quantum physics, indicated his liking for the kind of cosmological proposals being made by Dr Linde, and mentioned that some theological arguments (like preferring God as cosmic cause to an infinite regression of causes) arose more from classical than quantum physics. To my mind, this would weaken any attempt to use those arguments on the basis of the latest physics. And I left the interview quite clear that Dr Ellis definitely did not agree that the latest physics makes it more likely that there must be a personal creator than not. Informal discussions with other scientists support this impression.

Sceptics say that testimony like this deals a hefty blow at a favourite argument on the part of the believer. If the latest physics really does indicate that a personal intention explains the universe better than other theories, then surely we would find most experts in physics, if not all, agreeing with it. The plain fact is that the God-theory does not enjoy the kind of sustained support it would have among competent judges in the world of physics if it were as good an argument as believers think. That by no means makes it false. But it does mean that the believer's argument from physics is too weak to make theism rational. Stronger arguments will therefore be needed by the believers.

Biology and nature's evils

As we saw in the previous chapter, believers argue that the fantastic complexity of life from a single cell upwards cannot have evolved by sheer accident on this planet in the time available. There just hasn't been enough time for nature to experiment randomly and then, through trial and error, evolve life forms with all the features needed to survive in their particular settings, like moss in a cool, shady corner or polar bears in the frozen north. But, these believers go on to argue, if a blind process of chance is so unlikely, the more rational alternative is an intelligent cause which designed the system – in other words God.

If today's biology indeed makes a naturalistic version of evolution problematic, this should be accepted as giving grounds for entertaining the God-hypothesis. Wise sceptics then move on to a much more important objection (touched on briefly in the previous section), an objection based on what is sometimes called 'natural evil', along the lines of an argument worked out by the famous philosopher David Hume in the eighteenth century. They invite us to look soberly at all of nature and not just at the glowing sunsets and beautiful flowers so beloved by some sentimentalists as signs of God's alleged handiwork. They point out that a good deal of nature is indeed 'red in tooth and claw', a savage battlefield where life feeds violently on life in order to survive. They point to the crocodile seizing and drowning a thirsty antelope or small child for its next meal, and invite us to think for a moment about the sheer terror of that frightful experience, not to speak of the appalling physical pain of being gripped and lacerated by those deadly jaws as they violently shake their prey and drag it under the water.

Sceptics point out that there is a double problem here. Not only is there much destroying of life in nature by the strong against the weak, but large parts of the animal kingdom rely on pain to function. All living things can and will perish, and to survive long enough to reproduce requires – on the part of many species – a daily struggle to avoid whatever could harm or destroy the individual. For us humans and for many animal species, pain is a major tool for achieving this goal. It makes us pull back sharply from things that hurt, and then avoid them in future. Pain, in other words, is built into the system of animal and especially human life. Not only, then, does a living body which took years to form often face violent destruction by nature's hungry killers, but often it dies in a climax of the very pain that kept it alive. I myself once heard the wild, agonized cry of a man going to his death, and know exactly what the sceptics mean.

But there is even more they want us to notice about nature, namely the excrement, the pus, the disease and the putrefaction that are also part and parcel of it. Who can see these things and still entertain shallow, one-sided thoughts about the glories of nature? And with all this in mind, sceptics now ask the believer what is left of the theory that biology points open-minded people towards a perfectly loving divine creator?

It is vital that we grasp exactly what the objection here is. The quarrel is not with the idea that nature must have an intelligent designer with the vast power needed to turn his design into reality. The quarrel is with the further belief – absolutely essential to Christian theists – that this prodigiously intelligent and mighty designer is a being of the utmost love and goodness. Is it really credible, ask the sceptics, that a God like that would design the crocodile lurking near the banks as well as the thirsty little child who kneels down for a drink on a hot day, or design a life-system that is fuelled by pain, or all the other horrors of nature? This is of course the same question asked by the English poet William Blake in his famous poem 'The Tiger': 'Did he who made the lamb make thee?'

But we need not focus only on the animal kingdom. Sceptics remind us that people are born with different abilities. Some can run like the wind, others are slow of foot. Some are highly intelligent or otherwise 'gifted' (note the metaphor), while their fellows are born with modest minds and no great talent for anything. Some are big and strong, others small and weak. None of this is the result of human wrong-doing. If there is a creator, he must have willed these differences, and thus willed that some people are born with definite advantages over others. And since we all seem to have an inborn tendency to avoid pain and seek happiness, and since we feel our own pain and pleasure more acutely than that of other people, there is clearly also in us a capacity for self-serving behaviour. That, says the sceptic, seems to make God responsible for the basic injustices of life. Human evil has merely exploited the unequal distribution of ability which he ordains or at least tolerates, and is therefore a merely secondary factor causing the injustices all around us.

From these harsh, cruel aspects of nature sceptics draw an important conclusion, using the logical principle that a supposed cause must be like the realities it is intended to explain. (We would not be very impressed, for example, by the argument that a leaky new roof is the work of an expert builder doing his best.) So, because nature contains so much inherent suffering, destruction and ugliness, it is illogical to insist that it must have a perfectly loving and infinitely powerful architect and builder. Surely an architect with those qualities could easily have designed a life-system without all that hideous cruelty? Being all-loving, he would obviously want only the best. Being all-powerful he would be able to produce it. But what we actually have is far from the best, says the sceptic. Therefore the architect – if in fact there is one to start with – cannot be perfectly loving.

Pressing home the point, sceptics approvingly quote the biblical rule that 'by their fruits we shall know them'. They challenge the believer to admit that this rule must then also apply to whatever produced nature itself, with its mixture of the ugly and the lovely, the gentle and the cruel. Therefore they reject outright the argument that nature itself when realistically examined supports Christian faith in a God of perfect love as the alleged creator of a system containing so much pointless and vicious evil. Shakespeare speaks of history as a tale told by an idiot, full of sound and fury, signifying nothing. Radical sceptics tell us that a sober look at nature reveals either a meaningless mess or a tale devised by a sadistic genius, full of pain and horror, signifying cruelty. It knows nothing, they say, of an author who is gentle and kind.

Summarizing their response so far, these sceptics say that the appeal to philosophy turns out to be too highly speculative to produce reliable results, besides being heavily contested and quite possibly too ambitious to succeed. The appeal to biology turns out to create more problems for the God-people than it solves because it makes painfully obvious that whoever or whatever caused the cosmos – assuming it has a cause – is also responsible for the agony, cruelty and ugliness present in nature – which seems to clash head-on with perfect love. And the other pillar supposedly supporting the believer's bridge from unbelief to faith, namely physics, also turns out to be too weak to carry that bridge. To succeed, says the sceptic, these arguments would have to show that the God-hypothesis is at least somewhat more probable than other explanations of the universe. But it is no such thing. The best that can be said for believers here, say the sceptics, is that the experts are seriously divided about physics and God, for there are also senior physicists who think the cosmos does point towards a personal creator. But such division itself definitely weakens the believer's argument.

When we looked at the Christians' arguments we saw that while the appeal to Christ himself is said to give important, rational grounds for accepting God, it cannot stand on its own. It needs the support of independent arguments in favour of the God-hypothesis. Now, say the sceptics, we can see that believers are in fact wrong when they say that philosophy, biology and physics give them those further arguments. This in turn means their original argument based on Jesus lacks three of its main alleged, objective supports. What about the other arguments in that set, based on significant facts of human nature and culture? Do they tip the scales in favour of the believer?

Sceptics are convinced that they do not, as we shall see in the next sections.

Humanity as the product of nature alone

Sceptics are unimpressed with the idea that any of the characteristics of human life are more to be expected if God exists than otherwise. Accepting a modernized view of evolution, they point out that the only kind of intelligence that could endure in the harsh struggle to survive is one which is highly adapted to the world around it, and thus marvellously fitted to understanding that world. A mind that mistakes tigers or venomous snakes for harmless playthings is doomed, as we all know. Therefore there is nothing in the least puzzling, on naturalistic grounds, about human (or animal) intelligence being wonderfully adapted to an intelligible universe. Given an orderly but dangerous cosmos, the only kind of being with real prospects of surviving in it is one that is capable of learning what menaces it, and acting accordingly. The laws and principles of nature are enough to explain this fact, making the appeal to a divine cause unnecessary.

The same holds for self-transcending behaviour, according to the sceptic. One of the features of human intelligence is imagination – the ability to picture things that do not exist, for example things we might dream of having, like a way of easing pain. A being with this ability, which nature provides unaided through evolution, plus the ability to make things, which nature has also given us, is precisely also a being who will strive ceaselessly to turn those dreams of a better world into fact. The only effective counter to this argument would be to say with certainty that self-transcending achievements are beyond the scope of nature, and that has not been done by believers. So, says the critic, there is nothing problematic about treating the remarkable self-transcending ability of many people as a purely natural fact requiring no further explanation.

As for consciousness, which many believers regard as evidence that matter cannot be the only reality, here too the sceptics have their own theories. Some of them believe that the mind is none other than the brain, and that the difficulty we have in translating expressions which refer to our minds into ones which refer only to our brains is a problem of language, not a proof that there are two kinds of reality, matter and consciousness. Others, especially if they accept the theories of the philosopher A.N. Whitehead, regard the division of reality into material and mental things as itself an error. Instead, they think there is a mental aspect in everything. If so, then consciousness, as the highly evolved form of the mental aspect in all things, is something natural, not some mysterious extra thing injected into material bodies and therefore needing a non-material cause like a God. And then there are the monistic religious teachings of India which regard spirit or consciousness as the only true reality, and matter as a deceptive appearance. They too find no need for the notion of a divine creator to explain the origins of consciousness, for consciousness itself is a feature of reality at the deepest level. Thus we see that Christians have to contend with many plausible, rival theories about consciousness held by people no less thoughtful and informed than they. Sceptics argue that this considerably weakens the argument that consciousness needs a theistic explanation.

So far the objection has been that human nature needs no divine explanation, though it does not exclude it. Now we come to an objection of a seemingly more serious kind, namely that theism contradicts itself when it says that only by God's grace is true human fulfilment posssible. Sceptics making this objection point out that Christian doctrine teaches us that God not only exists but knows everything. That means he knows our inmost thoughts and everything else about us with perfect assurance. But how then can we ever be our real selves, for if such a God exists then there is never a moment's real privacy for anybody because God would know and see everything. That means that our lives are in fact never really our own; we live under the ceaseless glare of an invisible divine search-light, says the sceptic, under which every aspect of our existence is wholly visible to God. In fact he would know our motivations and everything else about us far better than we do. Does that leave us with any real space to be just ourselves? Doesn't it in fact make us like eternal infants in the divine eye, loving though it might be – on the analogy of parents who watch diligently over their children – only infinitely more so? But in that case it is nonsense to speak of true human fulfilment, the sceptic continues, for as children of an all-knowing deity we can never experience the privacy needed to grow into mature selves.

In view of these arguments, Christianity's secular critics conclude that human nature makes sense on its own as a product of nature, so that we do not need the God-hypothesis. Worse for the believer, according to them, they argue that true human well-being appears to be impossible if there is a God, which clashes outright with the central Christian idea that true fulfilment is only possible because there is a God. Since the promise of such fulfilment is central to Christianity and is also taught by the other religions, this is a convenient point to discuss the sceptic's view of the argument that religion itself is a strong pointer to the existence of a God.

Does religion itself mean there is a God?

The first blow against this belief is struck by Buddhists and others whose faith has no need of a God-concept. They point out that theists have never yet produced a theory of religion that does justice to non-theistic religion. After all, if one is sure the kind of God being discussed in this book really exists, then religions that make no reference to him must be seen as wrong. The Buddha and other great Eastern religious figures who found no need for that concept must then obviously also be wrong. But is it really likely that people of such mental, spiritual and moral power are indeed totally mistaken at the most basic level of their teachings?

We can perhaps understand that a Westerner who has never ventured out of the cocoon of Christianity might think this way. But nobody who has seriously studied the non-theistic faiths of India, China and Japan can rest easily with their being dismissed as simply mistaken. Why not? Because the literature and teachings of those faiths make it clear that they come from teachers and scriptures of the highest intellectual, moral and spiritual calibre, which makes it very unlikely that they could be so grossly blind as to cling to views which reason allegedly shows to be unsound. The very argument which believers in God use when they see his hand behind people like Moses, Jesus and St Paul – namely that these people and their numberless followers can hardly be dismissed as stupid, bad or mad – also applies to people like the Buddha and their followers. In fact there are even Christians who think that Buddhist teaching about ultimate reality has no peer among the religions, as we saw earlier. Certainly there can be no doubt about the deep compassion for all suffering beings that inspired his spiritual project.

It is of course true that there are more theists in the world than non-theists. But the latter are still a vast and very long-standing group, and sceptics insist that it clearly is far too simple to say that the good, thoughtful and intelligent folk of the West and the Middle East are largely (and even wholly) correct in believing there is a God, while the equally good, thoughtful and intelligent folk of China, parts of India and Japan are all wrong. The conclusion drawn by these critics is thus that Christian theism carries with it a clearly problematic account of those religions. It makes itself right and them wrong in a way that does not square with the facts about the people involved. It leads us to expect a degree of basic error in a faith like Buddhism which clashes with the clarity, depth of insight and spiritual power it in fact contains. But there is no other way for Christians, says the sceptic; they are logically obliged to view those religions as wrong, and that itself, says the critic, shows up the faultiness of their view of things.

In short, then, theism cannot appeal to the *facts* about religion on earth in support of itself without either falsifying the non-theistic faiths or changing the concept of God into something so broad (and non-personal) that it will no longer mean what theists have in mind with their God-talk. And that is precisely why increasing numbers of well-informed, open-minded Christian scholars know that traditional Christian belief about God is deeply problematic, and why they have begun the process of radically re-thinking it.

But this non-theistic objection is by no means all that can be said against theism so far as the facts of religion are concerned, seriously though sceptics think it damages the Christian case. There are other sceptics who see both of the two great forms of religion – those which have the concept of God and those which do not – as equally problematic because neither of them is thought capable of doing justice to the other. Each implies a basic wrongness in the other which clashes with the fact that both contain teachings of great insight, depth and persuasiveness, besides their respective, problematic aspects.

This gives rise to the verdict that no form of existing religion is capable of a valid explanation of the facts about religion. At this stage of the debate the secularists who acknowledge no reality beyond nature say that this inability of religion to explain itself is precisely what we should expect. There is no higher reality than the natural universe, according to them. All religion is thus seen as quite mistaken, and shows its error by being unable to do justice to the full facts about itself. That itself would tip the scales in favour not just of the non-theist but in favour of the secularist.

But doesn't this last contention repeat the same error we have seen on the part of believers? Isn't this merely another improbable claim that the good, thoughtful, intelligent religious majority of the world (and it is a vast majority) is quite wrong while the equally good, thoughtful and intelligent secularist minority is correct? In short, can secularists do any better at explaining religion than the believers they criticize?

We saw in the previous chapter that there are problems in the arguments given by the top secularists in this field, Feuerbach, Marx and Freud. But that does not mean a better, persuasive, naturalistic theory of religion is impossible, and earlier in this chapter I explained the main steps in today's feminist and naturalistic accounts of religion, the latter being a topic that is extensively discussed in my earlier book *Religion and Ultimate Well-Being*. What seems clear from the naturalistic world-view that was outlined earlier in the present chapter is that secularists are nowadays in a position to offer an explanation for religion which acknowledges the many strengths and great plausibility of theism and does not falsify its subject by implying that believers are basically neurotic, deluded or exploited, unlike the views of Freud and Marx. That is why they say that their explanation of religion makes far better sense than any other of the fact that among the world's good, informed and thoughtful people there are countless who are God-believing as well as many whose faith is non-theistic, and many others who are out-and-out secularists. If we add this to the fact that the critics of belief in God have exposed serious flaws in the argument that religion itself makes it more likely

that there is a God than not, then sceptics conclude that there is
plenty of justification for judging their account of religion much more
favourably than Christianity's.

In short, to the argument that it is more rational to think that sane,
decent, thoughtful, God-believing people are in touch with reality
than that they are deluded, the sceptic responds that it must then be
equally rational to think that sane, decent and thoughtful atheists,
non-theists and agnostics, as well as the many feminists who never
experience anything like a father-God, are just as much (or little) in
touch with reality. Clearly this conclusion is small comfort for people
who are convinced that traditional, orthodox Christian theism alone
is true. How could it help their cause to have to admit their rivals are
at least as rationally justified as they?

Even less acceptable to these sceptics is the further argument that
theism is sound because God himself has revealed its truth through
his prophets and the scriptures he inspires. They point out that this
would make God very unfair. It means he gives the priceless truth
only to certain favoured parts of humanity, not to all, keeping some
of the children he allegedly loves in the dark while giving light to
others. That hardly sounds like the ways of an infinitely and perfectly
loving God. This attempt to move the argument away from human
qualities to divine revelation is therefore regarded as self-contradictory, and we saw in chapter 1 that self-contradiction is a sure sign
that something is very much amiss.

Nor will it help to say that while God reveals himself equally to
all, some people just will not respond through either blindness or
badness. Nobody who has studied the facts can possibly accept such
a picture of the non-theist. It implies that some of history's noblest
people – whose love of truth and willingness to seek it open-mindedly
and earnestly is second to none – have knowingly and wilfully refused
to acknowledge that which is said to be the best of all realities. Who
could seriously entertain such a flimsy and even offensive notion,
asks the sceptic?

Secularists and members of the non-theistic religions argue that
they do not have to produce a flawless theory of religion to win this
round of the argument against the Christians. All they have to do is
refute or at least significantly weaken the claim that religion itself

provides grounds for theism, and give a non-theistic explanation of religion which is less problematic than its theistic rival. They say that this is precisely what they have done. The existence of deeply moral, sensitive, open-minded and caring people outside the ranks of the monotheistic religions is seen as a severe problem for believers in God because neither of their ways of explaining that fact works: neither the appeal to human error or wickedness, nor the appeal to divine revelation. This in turn means that Christian believers still have no convincing, independent case for saying that theism has reason on its side.

Thus sceptics conclude that the first five objective pillars of the believer's case – philosophy, biology, physics, human nature and religion itself – have all failed to stand up to the rebuttals of their opponents. But what of the remaining points made by the believer, namely that goodness of life, miracles and personal experiences of God give them the necessary objective support to win the debate? Let us take each of these in turn and see what the critics of theism say.

Doubts about God and morality

Everybody knows that Christians find Jesus of Nazareth morally inspiring and most non-Christians admire what they see as the high ethical standard of his life. There is also no quarrel with the fact that fine moral qualities and rare but real instances of conspicuous sanctity are present in Christianity. That is plain for all to see. What sceptics find problematic is the argument that these moral qualities arise because of the influence of God. They have three main objections to this argument. Firstly, what about the serious immoralities that are also part of the Christian story? Secondly, there is no evidence that Christians as a group are morally better than non-Christians. And thirdly, the examples of conspicuous sanctity that are present in Christianity can quite satisfactorily be explained, say sceptics, in purely human terms. They do not need a supernatural explanation at all.

In drawing attention to evils within the church, Christianity's critics are of course well within their rights. There can be no doubt that these exist. The women's movement has produced a mass of undeniable evidence about the way Christianity has discriminated against women and still does despite positive changes in some churches. As Mary Daly said in her book *Beyond God the Father*, 'if God is male, then the male is God' (p.7). And when men play god, women suffer. Just where is the 'good news' so central to traditional Christianity in such a situation? Why should women embrace something that promises liberation but produces bondage? Why indeed should fair-minded men embrace something that gives them unjust advantages?

There is an obvious parallel here between Christian sexism and Christian racism. In South Africa we have seen the injustice and cruelty of apartheid, a system created by people who have been steeped in the Bible and very loyal to Protestant Christianity. This is not a denial that very many other Christians like Desmond Tutu, Denis Hurley and Beyers Naude have tirelessly fought against apartheid. But we cannot allow our admiration for them to blind us to the evils that their fellow Christians have permitted and even encouraged, such as spending ten times more money on education for white children as for the black majority, or tolerating an economic system that has played havoc with the family life of black people and condemned most of them to lives of gross poverty and hardship.

As well as sexism and racism on the part of certain Christians there are other immoralities as well. A world famous environmentalist once told me that in his judgment Christianity had done enormous harm to the environment by teaching people that God had given them control over nature and commanded them to 'subdue' it. Nowadays we hear another story from enlightened Christians. We hear them giving a different interpretation to the biblical word 'subdue'. We hear of deep concern for the environment. This is a welcome trend but why was it so long in coming, asks the sceptic? Why was it not being firmly preached from every pulpit when the Industrial Revolution got under way and smoke stacks began belching their black clouds into the skies of England, Europe and America?

Examples of these evils could be multiplied. But the point is surely clear: in daily life Christianity is a mixture of good and evil. If God exists and imparts moral power to believers, then the good part is only to be expected, but what about the evil? Its prevalence erodes the Christian argument about God and morality because it implies that there is either something feeble about the moral power God is said to give to his devotees (since some of them show little sign of ethical enrichment) or that God doesn't give some Christians as much moral upliftment as others. Either way, he would then hardly be the perfect, almighty being he is supposed to be. In short, sceptics accuse believers once again of being selective in emphasizing the good in their religion and conveniently ignoring or trivializing the bad. As for the excuse offered by some conservative believers that there is a devil who causes the bad things, such reasoning merely convinces sceptics even more that these believers are deluded. After all, how can it possibly help their case to blame an alleged second supernatural being when we have yet to be convinced that the first one exists? And even if there is such a devil, he could only exist because God – who is alleged to be almighty and cannot therefore be forced into anything – lets him. In any case, continues the sceptic, we have yet to be given good grounds for concluding that this evil spiritual being exists anywhere other than in the imaginations of some believers. (This is of course by no means a denial that evil is real. Nobody doubts that.)

The point before us is very important. It certainly seems valid to say that if there really is a God of infinite love and power who cares utterly for us all as Christians say, then he would make the transforming power of his perfect goodness freely available to all, because we all need it. To use a simple analogy, a God of perfect love would obviously want only the best for his malnourished children. Seeing their plight he would certainly give them the moral diet they need. And if this God has chosen to channel that blessing to a needy world through Christ, the Bible and the church, then we would expect to find that this makes a real moral difference to all who have access to those channels, just as a vitamin-rich diet improves the health and well-being of those who have it. And if we then find that those people as a whole really are morally better than others, then we could conclude with some justification that a supernatural influence could perhaps indeed be at work here. But that is just the problem, says the sceptic, because we don't find a consistent or superior morality among Christians at all. And that in turn definitely justifies real doubts about the whole argument that goodness of life is another pointer towards the God believed in by Christians.

The second objection flows directly from the previous one, namely that there is no evidence that Christians as a group are morally better than non-Christians. The same is true of theists as a whole. Believers who have never met morally impressive non-believers are perhaps understandably ignorant of this fact. They remind me of the African proverb which says that those who never travel think their mother is the only good cook. But those of us who have had the good fortune to travel, culturally speaking, know only too well that the highest moral standards are to be found in people of every religious and philosophical persuasion, and that there is simply no basis for the notion that Christians are an ethical elite.

What does this fact do to the believers' argument? It is of course possible for them to reply that whenever goodness of life or great heights of holiness occur, there the Trinitarian God is at work irrespective of the beliefs held by the people in question. This sounds quite progressive and broad-minded. But in fact it weakens the specifically Christian case for faith in God very seriously, because the church has always insisted that God's saving grace is specially (and even solely) available through Christ, the Bible, the church and its teachings. Why else would he have become incarnate, founded the church and caused the Bible to be written? It is very illogical to insist on this point and then in the very next breath say that people outside the church can do just as well on their own or on the basis of non-Christian beliefs. Worse, it makes Christian belief ethically irrelevant, and it is hard to imagine a more fatal point for *believers* to concede. For one thing, such a concession makes the Christian doctrines of God and Christ a moral waste of time. And for another, it is simply not true that belief is ethically irrelevant. Some beliefs are true, others are false. Some are beneficial (like belief in fairness), others are harmful, (like belief in racial superiority). To imply that what we believe is ethically of no consequence is itself unethical.

Sceptics therefore conclude that there is nothing to be gained and much to be lost by Christians giving their God the credit for all human goodness irrespective of belief. They say their challenge remains unanswered: why are non-Christians who are not in touch with the alleged source of moral power ethically on a par with Christians, who supposedly are? The argument used by Christians means that their community *must* be both moral in its general character and indeed *more* moral than non-Christians. Neither of these reasonable requirements is met in practice, so the argument fails on these two counts already.

But there is still a third objection, coming from secular critics, namely that the rare but real examples of conspicuous sanctity among Christians (and other kinds of believer) require no supernatural explanation in the first place. It is enough, they say, that these people believe in a God who wants them to behave like that especially if he is thought likely to reward people for living according to his will, or to punish them if they don't. People are not uniform beings like peas in a pod. Some have lots of drive and determination, others less. Some persevere, others give up quickly when hardship comes. And a few, now and then, have exceptional abilities. When individuals with drive, determination and exceptional ability also believe strongly enough that there is a God who wants them to live a life of great self-sacrifice, and will perhaps bless them greatly in the hereafter when they dedicate themselves wholeheartedly to his will, then obviously we will occasionally find such people scaling the highest self-sacrificial mountains. That does not mean there is a God who gives them the power to do so. All it means, says the sceptic, is that a rare but perfectly possible set of purely natural conditions has been met. A notion does not have to be true to produce results. It is enough that somebody believes it. Racial superiority is false but its believers act as if it were true – and it then both changes their lives and hurts others.

So the sceptics conclude yet again that the believers' case is badly flawed and that no reasonable person who has outgrown the idea that one religious group stands morally higher than the rest, could seriously think that the moral characteristics of Christians give evidence that the God they believe in really exists.

The Case against the Believer

Refuting the appeal to miracles

Things are much the same with miracles. (There are sceptics who flatly refuse to accept that baffling healings and the like actually happen.) But that is bigotry, because open-minded people let their views be shaped by evidence, and clearly we do not have the evidence to say emphatically that events of a miraculous kind never happen. Wise sceptics therefore take the more sensible path of accepting that none of us knows everything, so that amazing events may indeed happen. Some go further and accept that such events have in fact happened. Where they differ from believers is in disputing the alleged divine cause of the so-called miracle.)

This disputing of the Christian explanation that miracles are God's work (as they understand God) has both a secularist and a non-theistic, religious form. As an example of the latter there are Hindus who say that the power to produce these baffling feats is acquired by spiritually advanced people who have learnt how to overcome the limitations of the world of matter. If this is so, then the supposed causal link between miracles and God, as defined by Christianity, is significantly weakened. An example of Hindu thinking on this matter is given in chapter 30 of the *Autobiography of a Yogi* by Paramahansa Yogananda, a chapter called 'The Law of Miracles'.

While noting this Hindu explanation let us also remember that God-believing Jews, Muslims and others have their own strong miraculous claims, like the exodus of the Hebrew slaves from ancient Egypt and the revelation of the Holy Qur'an. If Christian believers demand that sceptics heed evidence, then they themselves must also heed the evidence produced by those other theists. And the evidence is very strong indeed that Muhammed uttered a religious message which seems well beyond his own resources.) But accepting his message as God-given and miraculous is something mainline Christians cannot logically do because the Muslim message differs from the Christian one, so that they can't both be divine revelations and still mean what they say.

Christians paint themselves into a corner here, says the sceptic. Their own case – to their credit – rests very heavily on the principles of being led by good evidence and being logical. If they really respect these two principles they must admit that the amazing events for which other religions produce important evidence – like fire-walking or the message of the Qur'an – are just as likely to be God-caused as their own. This means that the miraculous channels God is said to work through must include those other religions, especially the revelation of the Qur'an, which conservative Christians would deny, none more so than evangelicals and fundamentalists. But, and this is much more serious for all mainline Christians, such a view would also mean that God gives humanity conflicting messages, because the teachings of the church and those of the Qur'an are incompatible in several crucial ways, most notably their respective pictures of Christ and salvation.

The theory by some Christians that miracles occurring outside the church are caused by evil spirits is, we have already seen in this chapter, deeply offensive to members of the other faiths, besides being an intellectually unsound argument, so there is no need to consider it again. When one is arguing that an alleged being (i.e. God) really exists, it is no use citing as part of the case an even more disputed, alleged being (i.e. the devil). The minority of Christians who nonetheless incline towards this argument should remember that their own scriptures say that to dismiss as evil that which is divine is an unforgivable sin; this might help them grasp the seriousness of dismissing as demonic the things other believers find sacred.

Turning now to the secularists, we find them opposing all brands of theism by saying that there are no sound, rational grounds for attributing miracles to a supposed deity in the first place. Arguing that none of the believer's previous arguments in favour of theism have proved sound, these people explain that we still have no rational grounds for accepting that God exists at all. Therefore it is asking far too much to cite him as the most likely cause of miracles. When we find that after prayers to God for help a desperately ill person recovers in a way that baffles the best medical experts, then all we are logically entitled to do is admit that we are at a loss to explain the event. Maybe a loving God caused it. Maybe unknown human or natural powers caused it. We just do not know and should accept our ignorance, not try to turn it into an irrational act of faith. To do the latter is merely to use the idea of God to fill the gaps in our knowledge. As plenty of believers know, that ploy tends to end badly for theism because human knowledge is forever growing, and the growth erodes the gaps – so making the concept of God more and more redundant.

Secularists also draw our attention to the modest nature of the miracles God is said by Christians to cause in our own day and age. We occasionally hear stories – which we need not doubt – about baffling recoveries from cancer or other unexpected benefits after people implore God to help them. For the people affected we would all rejoice. But why are there no large-scale miracles that would settle the matter for most of us, like preventing the terrible carnage of the World Wars, or of nuclear destruction? If there really is a God who loves us with an everlasting and almighty love, and who hates evil, why didn't he step in to stop the mass slaughter of Jews and other minorities by the Nazis? Why didn't he put an end to the evils of apartheid or of Stalin? Why did he let slavery, with its own terrible story, go on for thousands of years?

In short, the miracles the Christian God is supposed to cause give very few grounds, say these sceptics, for thinking that he is a perfectly loving and almighty being. They indicate sporadic, small-scale tinkering, and either indifference to or inability to overcome the large-scale horrors of history. As David Hume noted two centuries ago in another context, these sceptics add that we might have grounds here for detecting a junior deity, or one with very limited powers, or one who is less than perfectly good. What we cannot rationally claim is that miracles – those that we can prove happened, assuming there are some – reveal the all-perfect and almighty God spoken of by Christians. Why not? Because, as the same Hume also pointed out, when seeking causes we have to match the cause to its supposed effects. If it is illogical to watch a piece of paper blow gently off a table and say, 'Ah, a gale has sprung up,' then it is also illogical to mention a handful of baffling healings and the like and see in them the hand of an almighty God, unless we already have strong, independent reasons for thinking that such a God must in fact exist. But that is precisely what we do not have, say the sceptics, because every single argument put forward by the Christians so far has turned out to be unsound.

Believers who have not yet faced the worrisome logical implications of the notion that miracles add further weight to their position should study very carefully the opening chapters at least of Richard Rubenstein's book *After Auschwitz.* He is one of the very few theists (or former theists) who have grasped the moral problem of a supposed God whose hand is said to be the sovereign power over history, but who stays his hand when morality and compassion cry out in desperate anguish for help. After Auschwitz, says Rubenstein, there can be no question of believing in a divine, moral hand shaping history. The same point has struck others living amidst apartheid, whose evils over many decades were inflicted by members of a ruling elite which missed no opportunity to proclaim its loyalty to the Christian religion. If there really is a God with the qualities Christians talk about, a God who intervenes in the normal workings of nature to perform individual miracles, then how is it possible that he tolerated the evils of the apartheid state, ask the sceptics, especially as these were the work of people claiming to act in his name? How could he possibly remain aloof from such massive evil while his love and compassion were so flagrantly contradicted, given the fact (as believers see it) that he does from time to time perform miracles to help those who cast themselves on his mercy and compassion?

As these counter-arguments show, the sceptics have some very serious objections to Christians who think miracles help their case, which they say invalidate this particular part of the case for faith in God. We can therefore understand why some liberal church people find talk about miracles embarrassing. But secular-minded sceptics think there really is no way for Christians to avoid the problem of miracles, so long as they accept the historic teachings of their faith. They cannot drop the argument from miracles because miracles are a cornerstone of the New Testament tradition and of orthodox Christian teaching. Both of these insist that Jesus was raised miraculously from the dead and that he himself performed many miracles. So mainline, historic Christianity is committed to miracles. But that sets the scene for the counter-arguments we have just reviewed.

All in all, then, says the sceptic, it is impossible to avoid the conclusion that the critics of theism have succeeded in turning aside the apparent force of every argument put forward so far by the believer. Only religious experience and the facts about Christ remain to be considered. Open-minded enquirers, seeking the truth about Christianity's concept of God, are thus still standing on the sceptical bank. What they see of the alleged bridge, now that the sceptics have almost finished their critical testing, is a set of insecure pillars with only two still to be checked. Can they survive the test? And if they do, can they carry the whole bridge on their own? Let us see.

Problems with religious experience

Christianity's critics accept that some believers (including St Paul) occasionally have experiences which they think reveal the presence of God or Christ. But they argue that there is a better, non-theistic explanation of these experiences. The details are as follows. Firstly, the sceptics remind us that these experiences only seem to happen to people with the God-concept already in their minds. We don't hear about Zen Buddhists in Japan or members of the American Humanist Association suddenly finding their minds flooded with a sense that the God and Father of Jesus Christ is with them. Even St Paul fits this pattern because we know he was obsessed with the Jesus movement. The fact that his initial obsession was hostile doesn't alter in the least the fact that he was no newcomer to the name Jesus and what believers thought it stood for.

Next, we are reminded that existing concepts tend to act as moulds for new experiences, like looking at a drawing of three straight lines which meet at three points and saying, 'That's a triangle.' To be able to say that we must already know some geometry. Thirdly, we know that altered states of consciousness are possible. We know that 'mystical' experiences can be made to happen by certain chemicals and drugs. And we also know that we do *not* know everything about the brain. Therefore, say the sceptics, during times of serious stress or great joy people already convinced – even half-convinced – that God exists, or that Jesus cannot be ignored, could very well have experiences which strike them vividly as the presence of Christ or of God. The more deeply they have fixed those two concepts into their sub-conscious minds, for example by meditating or brooding intensely, the more likely it is that this can happen. When it does, it really tells us much more about the believer and his or her background than about a God who is supposed to exist outside the mind or an allegedly risen Christ, concludes the sceptic.

At the same time we can now see – so we are told – why Christian religious experience produces a vivid awareness of Christ, the Holy Spirit, the Virgin Mary and other objects of devotion in church circles, while Muslims in the same situation have experiences of Allah, Hindus of Brahman or Lord Krishna, and secularists like Bertrand Russell of a natural universe and no more. And – importantly – we can also see why secularists who have freed their minds of theistic ideas never have experiences of God but rather experience the absence of God, and why some believers with doubts about God who pray earnestly for him to make himself real to them, find the alleged divine doorway never opening in response to their anxious knocking, till in the end they finally decide that there is nobody at home and never was. All this makes perfect sense if there is no God, says the sceptic, but is deeply disquieting to the believer if there is because these facts – and they *are* facts – seem to be seriously at odds with the believer's world-view. After all, if there really is a God as Christians say, then how are we to explain the fact that the same type of experience happens in other religions, but has their character, not that of Christianity?

It does not look as if Christianity has a satisfactory answer to this problem, says the sceptic. If the Christian God causes all such experiences, and if it is important that people come to a saving knowledge of him in the form described by Christianity (as church people unquestionably say), then he seems to have seriously misled non-Christians by disguising himself so well in their religious experiences – an utterly unacceptable idea for the believer. And if the deity believed in by Christians does use those non-Christian concepts and is *not* misleading them, then clearly it is not important to think of him in the way Christians do. But that also flatly contradicts the teachings of the church. Obviously, orthodox Christians cannot argue like this. Perhaps they can argue that while their God definitely causes Christian forms of religious experiences, either evil spirits, or purely natural, mental processes causes them in other religions. But we have already seen how bad a thing, logically, it is to appeal to demonic causes; and to dismiss other religions' experiences of spiritual beings as purely natural, mental events, falls foul of three problems, says the critic. It raises all the old problems of apparent divine favouritism; it makes thinking people suspect that Christian religious experiences can just as easily be so explained; and it is intolerably insensitive to claim validity only for Christianity.

In any case, the sceptic continues, the experiences undergone by Christians are too few, too varied and too subjective to offer independent evidence that the existence of a God who causes them is likely. At most, they leave open a logical possibility that there might perhaps be something supernatural out there beyond our perception, something our own minds convert into the particular images described in the reports of religious experience. But on its own this is far too vague to justify the very specific belief in a Trinitarian God, and is thus not an argument which orthodox Christians could use.

These sceptical responses to the phenomenon of religious experience, added to the criticisms levelled at all the other arguments we have reviewed, lead Christianity's critics also to regard as subjective delusion the sense of inner, personal assurance which figures so largely in the lives of believers. Nobody doubts the sincerity of believers who say they have first-hand awareness of Christ or the Holy Spirit. But sceptics feel logically obliged to regard that awareness as the result of purely psychological and historical factors, because, so they say, we simply do not have enough objective grounds for treating theism as probable, whereas we do now have a plausible naturalistic explanation for the rise and persistance of the concept of God and thus for its profound influence over the minds of Christians.

So much for the critical response to religious experiences. While sceptics cannot claim that these experiences *must* be delusions, they have certainly cast doubt on the view that they are evidence for the Christian God. In the eyes of the sceptics, this obliges believers to fall back entirely on the facts concerning Christ in order rationally to justify their faith in God as Christians. But our study of those facts in chapter 2 suggested that on its own they are not enough to win the argument because they rest too heavily on the inconclusive, further argument that God must exist in order to have raised Jesus from the dead – assuming for argument's sake that he did in fact rise from the dead.

This means, says the sceptic, that the most that can now be claimed by Christians is the modest argument that the facts about Jesus and some of the other arguments used by believers provide tentative grounds for theism, but these are not strong enough to justify the notion that theism is closer to the truth than its rivals. The *best* possible result for Christians would thus be a draw, but that is a far cry from the confident belief of some Christians that reason itself plus the facts are their greatest ally. Small wonder, then, that perhaps the most influential of modern Christian theologians, Karl Barth, argued passionately that faith and not rational argument was the way to God through Christ. Perhaps he sensed what sceptics claim to have shown – that Christians do not in fact win a rational debate about the existence of God, though we have not yet been shown that they lose it either.

A drawn debate – which sceptics say is the most that Christians can hope for at the present stage of our investigation – would mean that Christian faith in God is neither more nor less rational than its rivals. So long as Christians can appeal to solid facts about Christ and plausibly argue that God is the best explanation for those facts and also for things like the existence of the universe and its orderliness, such a draw is possible and they are still in the race. Put the other way around, this means that the sceptic must now refute the Christian appeal to Christ in order to win the debate.

A naturalistic view of Christ

As we have already seen, most secularists find the ethical qualities of Jesus Christ deeply impressive. Moved by his compassion for those who suffered and his friendship with people whom society by-passed, and filled with admiration for his courage in taking the stand he did against such powerful foes, a courage extending to death itself, these secularists readily accept the verdict of Humphrey Carpenter at the end of his book called *Jesus*, that 'in the field of moral teaching his forcefulness has had no equal'. They also see no good reason for doubting that he had – and used – a rare gift of healing. Taken together with the appeal of his message about a heavenly father who cares utterly for his children and his moral stature, that gift makes it easy to understand why he quickly won a wide following among the poor and powerless in particular, with an inner core of deeply dedicated followers who would carry his movement into the future after his death. Similarly, secularists have no trouble in explaining why Jesus also earned for himself the bitter hostility of many of his fellow Jews. Anyone who claimed the right to forgive people's sins and to give his own corrections of the Law of Moses, which Jews see as God's most precious gift to the world, would naturally offend and deeply anger many around him.

Thus, says the sceptic, the general outline of Jesus' story fits easily into a naturalistic framework. A man naturally gifted as a healer and teacher, vividly speaking of his vision of an eternally loving God whose power was even then touching the world, and bravely enacting it for all to see in a world of deeply-held Jewish piety occupied by Roman troops edgy about unrest, such a man would obviously win dedicated followers but also make deadly enemies. That this pattern should lead to his death at the hands of his enemies as well as leading to a group of followers too deeply affected by him to let it all die away, is exactly what any thoughtful person would expect. There is no need, say these secularists, to call on supernatural factors when natural ones work as well as this.

But the Jesus story obviously does not get its power from the broad pattern of his life. Its power comes from two additional and very specific factors – Jesus' own conviction that there truly is a loving heavenly father with whom he personally was in the closest contact and whose power flowed through his hands in acts of healing, and secondly his followers' belief that he had been raised from the dead as an act of God which vindicated his life's work after the horrifying events of his arrest, torture and public execution. The acid test of a convincing, secular account of Jesus is how it copes with these two factors.

As for the first one, secularists argue that there is nothing at all puzzling about Jesus being a theist. We saw earlier in this chapter that their naturalistic world-view provides a plausible explanation

of the rise of the God-concept, born – once humanity had tumbled
to the principle of cause-and-effect – of a natural puzzlement at what
might make the great imponderables of life happen, like sudden
disasters or windfalls, coupled with an equally natural and unconscious tendency to model the unknown world on the known, in this
case on the human. Jewish culture was one of many where this
natural path to a belief in one or more mighty but unseen beings had
taken such deep root that it was universally and unquestioningly
accepted. From infancy onward, children would therefore have a
belief in God implanted in their trusting young minds by those they
loved and knew best, their parents, brothers and sisters and other
close relatives. With nothing in their own culture to challenge or even
contrast realistically with theism, it is clear that everybody would
share a basic faith in the God they believed had shaped and guided
their history. Thus Jesus also believed unwaveringly in that deity,
just as naturally and unwaveringly as people today believe in demo-
cracy or electrons.

Thus equipped by his culture with a basic belief that there is a God
who created the world, who loves his people as a father loves his
children (a notion that had long been present in the teachings of the
Hebrew prophets), Jesus' own creative genius as a religious teacher
and healer then naturally took on its distinctive God-orientation. His
beliefs about God become factors unconsciously shaping his own
experiences. This well-known psychological feature of our thinking
processes – in which we see things in the light of prior conditioning
– was explained earlier in the present chapter and has been extensively
discussed by thinkers like Ludwig Wittgenstein in his *Philosophical
Investigations* and by John Hick in his book *Faith and Knowledge*.
A person already deeply conditioned into the belief that there is a
God who is the giver of all good things (including punishment when
necessary), will experience the discovery of a remarkable healing
talent as a gift of God. And a sense of the marvellous way the lilies
of the field are sustained will be felt, naturally and unconsciously at
that time, as God's caring presence in nature, not as the result of
soluble soil nutrients and osmosis in an ecologically stable environment.

Thus secularists, accepting that Jesus had a remarkably rich and creative sense of a deeper, fuller dimension to life, of a crowning but entirely natural goodness pervading all things (as these secularists would put it), find no problem in Jesus seeing what he saw as the loving presence of God. Nor is there any real mystery about his own reported sense of being in the closest contact with the heavenly Father; what else would he feel as he experienced a unique power of healing flow from his hands to those in pain or distress? What else would he feel as he came to see that his was a religious sense that went far beyond that of others around him for depth, insight and inspiring power? Those of us who have studied reports of modern-day religious experiences, or had them ourselves, know that these experiences bring about an unmistakable change of consciousness, as though we had changed gear upward to a higher plane of awareness marked by peace, deep insight and joy. To know that is to sense powerfully that one is much closer to the mysterious source of all that is good, true and beautiful – whether that is a God, some other spiritual reality, or just the heart of nature itself. And if these experiences happen again and again in a way that one realizes is not shared by others, then it becomes perfectly natural to believe – without arrogance or pretence – that one has a special closeness to the source of it all. And that is exactly why Jesus could think of himself (as he reportedly did, though we have no first-hand evidence), as being exceptionally close to what he experienced as the heavenly Father who was acting in and through his own life and message.

In view of this naturalistic portrait of Jesus, secularists understandably reject the famous 'trilemma' which some conservative Christians use when arguing that Jesus must have been divine. Anybody who taught that he was intimately and uniquely close to God must be either God, mad or bad, we are told. And since Jesus was neither mad nor bad, he must have been God. Sceptics find this a mere debating trick, like asking somebody if he still cheats on his income tax return, because it suppresses other ways of explaining Jesus – such as the secularists' idea that Jesus was genuinely a deeply spiritual person whose social conditioning made him interpret his own religious experiences in the best way available to him – as God's own inspiring presence in his life. The trouble with the trilemma, in short, is that it is too shallow and simplistic to meet the rich subtleties and complexities of the real world. Worst of all, says the sceptic, it can't even do justice to the facts about Jesus, which it was intended to do.

Now we must see how secularists (and indeed some liberal Christians like Lloyd Geering in his book *Resurrection: A Symbol of Hope*) account for the second of the two factors behind the Christian faith, namely the belief in Jesus' resurrection as an act of God. Let us remind ourselves of our finding in chapter 2 that the evidence leaves the enquirer midway between accepting that Jesus did rise and scepticism; the evidence is too good to be dismissed out of hand but too problematic to be accepted either. Secularists say that there really is no obligation on them to explain anything here, because believers have not established that Jesus probably did rise from the dead. Maybe he did, but then again maybe he did not. Add this to the problems that sceptics expose in all the other Christian arguments in favour of theism, and the total picture is found to be so unfavourable to the believer that some sceptics think we are now justified in concluding that there was no bodily resurrection at all. We may well have real problems explaining how the belief that Jesus had in fact risen and that his tomb was empty originated in the first place, but that is easier for a rational person to live with than to conclude that there probably was a resurrection caused by God when the grounds for believing in a God are as shaky as they are. In fact those grounds, says the sceptic, amount to no more than the problematic resurrection tradition itself, because everything else put forward by Christians has been effectively answered by their critics.

While most radical sceptics argue this way, some others respond to the resurrection question differently. They grant – even if only for argument's sake – that Jesus really did rise from the dead but say that it is more rational to seek the cause of that amazing happening in natural or paranormal powers we do not yet understand, than to say there must be a God who caused it. The Hindu argument about the miraculous powers allegedly possessed by very spiritually advanced people, which we have already noted, is an example of this reaction. If this is what happened – and it would fit well with the longstanding biblical tradition that the tomb of Jesus was found empty despite having been under an official guard – then it is certainly easy to see why Jesus' disciples were convinced that God had raised him. Their thinking as Jews would have followed the same pattern as that of their leader, so that the natural, and indeed automatic and unconscious reaction for them to seeing the risen Jesus when he appeared to them would be to interpret the event as an act of God – by far the best explanation open to them. Given an understanding of conceptual relativity, we can even say that such an explanation was the soundest one in that situation. But, say the sceptics, a wider knowledge of things shows up the problems in it and invites us to find better explanations.

There is also a third sceptical way of trying to account for the belief that Jesus rose from the dead. Once again it is denied that we have enough grounds for believing that there was a bodily resurrection. What really happened, according to this version, was a series of visions of Jesus by his closest followers, much like modern religious experiences by people who say they have had visions of Christ. Those earliest disciples, having gone through the immense emotional upheavals of passionately and devotedly following him and then seeing him arrested and brutally crucified, would be just the kind of people in whose ranks this kind of experience is most likely. Given the further point that some of them already believed that God in his justice would raise the righteous from the dead, it would be quite natural for them to experience those visions as resurrection appearances, and thereby come to believe that Jesus had triumphed over death through God's almighty hand. Similarly, spiritualists (who believe that we have a sort of spiritual or 'etheric' body as well as our physical one, which lives on automatically after death) explain the resurrection as a series of appearances of Jesus from the spirit world. Once again there is no recourse here to the idea that a God must have been at work.

As for the tradition that the tomb of Jesus was empty, the reply is that this is in any case a secondary, later tradition, a point accepted by a good many sophisticated biblical scholars. Our oldest source is Paul, who knows nothing of it – an amazing piece of ignorance in one who consulted Peter himself, who, according to that later, empty-tomb tradition, saw it for himself. If that is so, says the sceptic, it is truly incredible that he never impressed that fact (if so it was) on Paul. This suggests to sceptics that the tomb was in fact never empty, or at least not empty because the body of Jesus had been raised, and that a later tradition formed (as these things often do) on the basis of those visionary experiences of Jesus *and of the existing Jewish belief in bodily resurrection*, to the effect that since he was alive and was thus 'risen from the dead', this also meant that his physical body had been raised and that his tomb must therefore have been empty.

By these means those who dispute the Christian view of things claim to have shown, on the basis of a wider set of factors than the ones which most Christians emphasize, that we have virtually nothing to make it more rational to believe that there is a God than the converse. Even the central Christian appeal to Jesus is said to fail because a naturalistic account of him allegedly makes more sense than the familiar theistic one, incomplete though it may be at present. He emerges as an unforgettably compassionate person and a superbly inspiring ethical and religious teacher with an undyingly noble vision of all things finding their fulfilment in love, a vision he naturally clad in the theistic concepts of his time and culture. But, concludes the sceptic, just as we no longer invoke God to explain the weather or the tides, so we no longer need that notion to do justice to the facts about Jesus, or to the validity of his essentially humane (and wholly human) vision.

Overcoming Christianity's great self-contradiction

Having explained how they interpret Jesus, sceptics turn now to their final objection to traditional Christianity. It deals with something which these critics (and even some Christians) think Jesus himself never held or taught but which his followers in later generations evolved into a central dogma of the church. This is the belief that Christ is the incarnate Son of God, second person of the Holy Trinity, in whom a divine nature united with a perfect human nature and who was sent into the world by God the Father as *the only saviour*. Those who repent and accept him will have eternal life, while those who do not will be eternally lost, a view which many Christians have traditionally interpreted as meaning eternal damnation, to which humanity is said to be justly headed because of its sinfulness.

Sceptics say this notion flatly contradicts the basic point taught by

Jesus himself, namely that God's love is everlasting and perfect, so that it cannot possibly be true. But in that case neither can traditional Christian theism as a whole be true because its distinctive character comes precisely from this belief in an incarnate Son of God who is the only way to salvation. Sceptics both secular and religious think that their view of Jesus as a great and noble human being and not a God in human form gets rid of this seemingly glaring self-contradiction in the doctrines of the church, one which is also alleged to do great harm to what is ethically best in that religion – its emphasis on love as a power capable of radically changing human existence for the better – by shackling it to so problematic a belief.

What is contradictory about Christianity at this point? Sceptics argue firstly that it is nonsense to say that humanity is justly headed for eternal damnation because of its sinfulness. Where is the justice of eternally punishing even the most wicked person? We think poorly of those former days when a thief could be sentenced to death for stealing a sheep because the penalty is far too severe for the crime. Why should we then think well of an even worse imbalance in the religious sphere? The nineteenth-century philosopher Arthur Schopenhauer vigorously attacked this notion in some memorable words which are worth quoting. In his essay 'The Christian Symbol' he wrote, 'a punishment which comes at the end of all things, when the world is over and done with, cannot have for its object either to improve or to deter, and is therefore pure vengeance' (*The Essential Schopenhauer* p. 19). The God spoken of by Jesus cannot possibly act like that if he in fact exists, says the sceptic, so there is no rational or ethical basis for thinking that humanity is damned in the first place. That in itself cuts away the ground under the whole idea that we urgently need a saviour, say these critics, dealing a massive blow to the Christian doctrine that God himself has ordained that accepting Christ is the only way to salvation for the world.

But, says the sceptic, let us grant for argument's sake that we are all justly headed for damnation and do therefore urgently need God's help. In such a situation a God of perfect love would certainly throw out a lifeline to a drowning humanity, but there is absolutely no way he would do so for just a favoured minority of people. Yet that is exactly what the orthodox, traditional Christian doctrine of salvation allegedly implies by insisting that Jesus is God in human form whom we must accept as our only saviour if we want to have eternal life, either through membership of the church or through a conscious act of faith in him. Given the cultural and geographical realities of the world, there simply is no way a lifeline in the form of a unique, divine incarnation could possibly reach more than a minority of those who need it, even in our own day of global communications. The result is that the majority drowns because it is out of reach of the lifeline through no fault of its own. But that cannot possibly be how a perfectly good and just God, who is also almighty, would operate, says the sceptic. But if it is (as most Christians evidently think), then it is hard to deny Schopenhauer's sardonic remark that 'it looks as if the Blessed Lord . . . created the world for the benefit of the devil' – who obviously walks off with the bulk of humanity according to this view of things.

There is also a further problem according to Christianity's critics. If a divine saviour really was necessary, then obviously humanity must have got itself into such a serious mess that it needed supernatural help. But the mess can only have come about through two causes: human evil arising from the misuse of our freedom, and natural evil proving too much for us to handle. But where did *they* come from in the first place? According to Christian doctrine, from God, because he gave us that freedom and he designed nature. Surely, says the sceptic, this must mean (as the philosopher David Hume once argued), that the original design of both humans and nature was faulty; it led to such severe problems that the creator had to step in as saviour to correct things. If that creator was perfect, why were humans given too much freedom and nature too much destructiveness in the first place?

The last aspect of this criticism of inconsistencies in Christian theism by sceptics is also about human freedom. We saw in chapter 2 how essential it is for Christians to insist that humans really do have a genuine freedom, for otherwise they cannot hope to solve the problem of the presence of evil in a world created by a perfect God. But, asks the sceptic, just how free was the human nature of Jesus Christ, if – as orthodox doctrine holds – that human nature of his was destined even before conception to be united with a divine nature as the incarnate Son of God? The Gospels say that God willed this to happen and that an angel conveyed his intention to Mary, who accepted it. She may thus have had some choice in the matter, but Jesus, considered as a truly human being, seemingly had none. Does that not contradict the idea that he was the ideal human being? Once again, says the sceptic, orthodox doctrine proves fraught with problems, whereas a naturalistic account of Jesus explains all the genuine facts without those contradictions, and is thus much more likely to be true.

So critics discern what they see as some glaring inconsistencies at the heart of the distinctively Christian doctrine of God. That means it must be mistaken, they say. There could be a perfect God, and there could be a God who gives himself as saviour to a favoured minority. What there cannot be is a God who is both. In other words, says the sceptic, Christians speak of a God whose main action after creating the universe, namely entering history in Christ to offer salvation to the few who are near enough to hear the message, contradicts his own nature and motives as an almighty God of everlasting and perfect love. Therefore he is either not a perfectly loving and almighty God in the first place, or he didn't enter history as the church says he did. Either way, says the sceptic, the distinctively Christian view of God as exclusively embodied in Christ who is the only saviour, is irrational.

Therefore sceptics are sure that the Christian believer is wrong about God. Coupled with all the other problems we have seen, this leads them to end their side of the debate by saying that they have conclusively refuted the Christian case for faith in God. Not only are Christians very mistaken about how they think a perfectly loving God would act, namely by ordaining that humanity must perish eternally for its sins and then personally entering history in Christ to offer salvation in a manner which cannot possibly be fair to all; they are just as mistaken in thinking there is one to start with because every argument they give in support of that belief turns out to be dubious at best.

In short, sceptics – secular-minded ones above all – deny that Christianity has even earned itself a creditable draw. The attempt to show by rational and factual means that faith in the Trinitarian God is the soundest world-view has been, they say, decisively refuted. Are they correct? If so, would that mean that there is no God? In the next chapter we will identify the conclusions that seem to flow most logically from the arguments we have reviewed in the two main chapters of this book, and thereby reach an answer to these questions.

4

Judging the Debate

In this final chapter we reach the climax of our investigation. The issue here is the verdict about the existence of God that would be reached by people who genuinely and open-mindedly seek the truth by weighing all the evidence as carefully and fairly as possible and by reasoning logically. The best way to reach such a verdict is to assess each argument in turn as well as judging the cumulative merits of the two main belief-systems we have been hearing, so arriving in the end at a verdict on the total world-views built respectively from those arguments.

In the two previous chapters we heard two rival stories about the nature of things. They cannot both be true because they clash head-on. We have heard the Christian story with its central idea of a perfectly loving and almighty God who is the bedrock of reality and the source of all goodness, a Trinitarian God who created all things, giving human beings a genuine measure of creaturely freedom and responsibility, and who entered history personally in Jesus Christ as the only saviour of a world said to be justly headed for damnation as the punishment for sin. We have heard the many objections to this story, or to key parts of it, by secularists as well as by members of the other religions, even those who also believe in a God. And we have heard the rival story of the most radical of Christianity's critics, the secularists who judge all religion to be false and harmful. Now we must judge which side has the stronger case and thus arrive at a verdict about whether the God spoken of by Christians really exists.

This concluding act of deciding the outcome of the debate is an exceedingly complex matter. The points involved are themselves seldom easy or straightforward and there simply is no agreed way of ranking them relative to one another. Nor can we ever completely set aside our own personal interests, backgrounds and limitations as we try to distill the implications of the debate. For that reason this book has been written in such a way that readers are now in a position to weigh the various arguments for themselves, having had the agreed rules of debate explained and all the relevant evidence presented as fairly and vigorously as possible. Nonetheless, it would be a serious mistake to dismiss the whole matter as purely subjective, for clearly there are objective factors here, in the form of agreed evidence and logical patterns of argument. These are by no means merely personal. The criteria which come into play are ones which any thoughtful person can see are appropriate and fair – clarity, supporting evidence of the kind we can all, in principle, investigate for ourselves, logicality and moral value.

Even so, there is no denying the complexity and difficulty of trying to judge the debate about God as objectively as possible. What follows is my own version of that judgment. In giving it my aim is to provide an example of one person's way of wrestling with this vital question and thereby encourage others to do the same and to reach whatever conclusions the evidence seems to them logically to warrant. The more informed debate there is about the existence of God, the better. These points having been made we can now proceed to the task of judging the debate.

What is the ultimate reality?

We start with the philosophical dispute about ultimate reality. The issue here is whether, on balance of probability, the natural universe around us – in the widest possible sense which would include all universes if there are other ones than our own – can be accepted as the only reality, or whether it is more rational to infer that the universe depends on something else for its existence, namely God. This is not a dispute about the facts of science, for both sides accept those facts. Instead it is a dispute about the philosophical status of the universe: can it rationally be seen as self-sufficient and complete in itself, or not?

Favouring the believer is the principle of the greater prior likelihood that something simple will be the basic reality, rather than something complex, for God is defined as an exceedingly simple kind of reality whereas the universe is very complex. Confining ourselves to just this single principle, it follows that it is more likely that a God would be the ultimate reality than the physical universe. But on the other hand, we know that the universe exists, whereas the existence of God is a matter of very real dispute among competent judges, and from the lesser logical probability of the universe being the ultimate reality it does not follow that it cannot be such. Maybe, at this deep level of things, matters are not as neatly logical as they are elsewhere. And perhaps we must take care not to exaggerate the complexity of the cosmos. Perhaps science will succeed in giving us a grand, unified theory in which the whole unfolding universe and its seeming complexity would be traced back to a unified, harmonious, and much simpler condition or force. In that case the scales would tilt away from the believer to a verdict that is less unfavourable to the secularist. And as for the kalam argument, we saw in chapter 3 that this cannot be judged as tipping the scales significantly in favour of the believer, though it seems to me to be a valuable part of the believer's cumulative case. It relies too much on ordinary experience (and on pre-quantum physics) to reach really strong conclusions about something as remote from ordinary experience as cosmic origins.

Nor can we neglect at this point the important objection by Jews, Muslims and others who dispute Christianity's Trinitarian view of God, for clearly theirs is an even more simple concept of the deity. That gives their view of God greater prior probability than Christianity's view, all other things being equal. But Christians are convinced that other factors (chiefly their view of Jesus Christ) swing things back their way, which shows that Christians cannot consistently demand that the principle of the greater likelihood of the simple is a decisive factor. Nor can we overlook rival religious theories about the ultimate reality, such as the Hindu idea of Brahman or the Chinese idea of Tao, though they are not the focus of debate here. But they do allow us to see that although the Christian view that God is the ultimate reality has greater intrinsic or prior probability, being very much less complex, than the secularist's view that nature is ultimate, there are other religious concepts of the ultimate reality which enjoy even greater simplicity. And it is by no means inconceivable that some fertile thinker, mindful of the facts of both religion and physics, will produce a new concept of even greater logical simplicity to regard as truly ultimate.

But even though these are valid points, the fact remains that *at the present stage of our knowledge, the cosmos is too complex to be a likely brute fact, so that it probably stems from something much simpler and capable of causing it, such as the God believed in by Christians,* all other things being equal between the two rival world-views, which they are at this initial stage of judgment, but with things being rather less favourable to Christians than to the other monotheists and religious monists with their even simpler concepts of ultimate reality.

However, the overall force of this argument must not be exaggerated because it is entirely theoretical. It does not prove that there is a God, and it does not make atheism or agnosticism irrational. On the other hand, it does indicate that believers open their case with an argument which so far shows theism to be a highly rational position and definitely not the irrational thing some critics dismiss it as being. Whether the more specific factors dealt with in the next arguments allow theism to retain or even increase this rational probability remains, of course, to be seen.

Valuably for the believer, the argument about what is ultimate operates at the most general level of all, because it deals with the nature of the universe as a whole. Grounds for supporting the God-hypothesis at this all-embracing level strike me as counting more than grounds at a very localized level, such as a single isolated event, because they imply that the bare fact of existence on the part of all things whatsoever is such as to make the God-hypothesis more likely than its secular rival. Single, localized phenomena do not have such sweeping implications, and if they do clash with a theory, can thus more plausibly be treated as isolated puzzles which do not refute the theory in question.

Judging the Debate

What about God and modern science?

The arguments based on the findings of modern physics are not as general and abstract as the ones we have just evaluated, but they are still very broad in scope because they embrace the entire physical universe. At issue is why this universe, or at least our part of it, with its evident big bang beginnings, had precisely the right structure to lead to intelligent life, when very many other structurings were possible which would not have led to such life. The odds against such a situation happening by chance alone are enormously high, making that a very unlikely explanation on rational grounds, whereas the power of an intelligent and almighty creator would give us a very plausible explanation.

But as we saw in chapter 3, sceptics insist that we should consider the full picture of the cosmos, which includes natural evil, and not just limit ourselves to the phenomenon of intelligent life, so let us take the results of physics and biology together. This discloses a universe with precisely the right ingredients, in precisely the right proportions, to produce from the big bang not just an awesomely orderly and complex cosmos but also a statistically very unlikely system of life on this planet at least, which on the one hand contains the marvels of intelligence, consciousness, artistic creation and moral behaviour, but on the other hand also contains, no less inherently, a vast drama of pain, violent destruction, ugliness and tragic death, some of it at least serving no evident positive purpose but merely crushing the helpless creatures caught up in it.

What is the more likely explanation for such a universe, containing a planet like ours with both a complex bias towards life and much natural evil – nature alone or a divine creator acting out of his perfect love? The evidence in this case points in different directions. The odds against such an astonishingly life-orientated, highly structured and orderly universe occuring by chance alone are so high that fair-minded, rational enquirers will surely concede that the God-hypothesis is a far more likely explanation of that fact – unless there is more to nature than science has yet uncovered, for example some kind of inherent, natural bias towards life as a brute fact. That is always possible, and should caution believers against relying too much on areas where our scientific knowledge is incomplete. This alone introduces an element of doubt about the seemingly strong indications of divine creation cited by the believer. But even so, the rationality of saying that the complex, orderly structure of our universe points with greater probability to an intelligent and almighty creator than to mere chance should be clear to all. Thus the theists once again have a more rationally impressive case than their secular rivals at the present stage of our knowledge. Taken together, these first two arguments based on philosophy and physics reinforce each other and tip the scales of probability even further in favour of the believer.

On the other hand there is the appalling fact of natural evil, a reality that is undeniably vast, pervasive and relentless throughout the animal kingdom especially, including human existence. It has been argued that without plenty of natural evil, people would never learn moral responsibility, which is so great a good that it justifies that evil. But for many, such a verdict is unconvincing. It implies that a perfectly loving God creates the vast system of nature and its untold miseries as no more, in effect, than a trial ground for human beings, which strikes many of us as an unacceptable and dangerous instance of human-centredness of the kind that has done great damage to nature already. And it also seems to many of us that the amount of suffering is in any case far greater than is needed for humanity's moral growth.

There is of course no objective way of measuring this surplus of pointless suffering; we as judges must draw whatever conclusion seems to us to be valid provided we all look the facts of natural evil fully in the face and acknowledge just how vast this reality really is. Having done so, we must ask how likely it is that such a cosmos could be the handiwork of a perfectly *loving* and almighty creator of the kind described by orthodox Christians of all kinds, a creator who is said to give the cosmos its basic characteristics at least, and the rational conclusion, surely, is that this is unlikely. Some would even say it is impossible; for them, the concept of God dies in the jaws of the crocodile. But others, myself included, draw a less harsh conclusion from their reading of the same facts. For us, the jaws of the crocodile seriously wound rather than destroy the mainline,

Christian view of God, and make it very heavily dependent on other arguments to overcome that wound. Our reason for drawing this less harsh conclusion comes from the way we assess the relative force of the issues before us – on one hand the vast and awesome orderliness of the entire known universe and its amazing bias towards intelligent life, and on the other the horrors of natural evil affecting especially the animal kingdom on this planet. Clearly, at the present stage of our knowledge the former is a much more widespread reality than natural evil, and its vastly greater scope strikes us as carrying more weight than the comparatively localized problem of natural evil, serious though the latter most certainly is.

Nonetheless, it still seems clear that far from being strongly indicative of a divine creator, the world of nature as revealed by modern physics and biology produces an ambivalent conclusion at this point in our judgment. The orderliness of the entire known universe and the odds-against complexity of life favour an intelligent, prodigiously powerful personal creator as their cause rather than being a brute fact of nature, but the enormity of nature's pointless evils – pus, predation, pain and putrefaction on a very great scale – seems to be severely at odds with the supposed character of that creator as a loving being who made each thing what it is, or at least wills them to be what they are. That in turn counts against the traditional Christian story of a divine creator. It is important to grasp that this traditional view is not just found among biblical fundamentalists in the Protestant churches, but is very widely held in all parts of Christianity, including the Roman Catholic church. According to the book *Aquinas* by the authoritative Catholic writer F.C. Coplestone, the same basic view is taught by that most imposing of Catholic theologians, Thomas Aquinas, who held that 'every finite thing depends existentially on God at every moment of its existence' and that 'God eternally willed that out of all possible worlds this particular world should begin to exist in such a way that the temporal order is what it is' (pp. 142, 144).

The counter-argument by some believers that natural evil is ordained by God as punishment for the moral evils he foresaw that people would commit cannot do much for Christians here. Where is the justice of making animals suffer for human evil, or babies suffer because adults are sinful? Where is the justice when a good and caring person dies in an earthquake or flood? So we are left with the serious problem of reconciling the fact of excessive natural evil with the idea of a perfectly good and loving God who intended that the present universe should exist.

This problem is especially evident in connection with any version of Christianity which teaches that God controls everything in a direct manner, for in that case his invisible hand pulls every lever of pain in a way that seems impossible to reconcile with the message Jesus Christ gave of a loving heavenly Father. But we have already seen that the Christian doctrine of God does not always have this emphasis, and at its best (in my judgment), it places the emphasis clearly on the idea of a loving God who therefore gives his creatures the inestimable gift of freedom, and it is this latter version of mainline Christian theism that is at issue in the present debate, not the other one. But in view of the prevalence of that other version, I will occasionally discuss its merits as we proceed.

Returning now to the God-concept of Christians who define God's nature chiefly in terms of love, the divine gift of freedom is usually taken to refer to human freedom, where it means that God does not directly cause or control everything in our lives. Instead, he gives us our autonomy, like a wise parent with a maturing child. That is the essence of the freewill defence cited by believers when asked how God can allow people to inflict so much evil. But it seems possible to extend this emphasis on freedom from human nature to nature as a whole, and say that God creates an autonomous, self-determining universe by setting certain broad and basic characteristics in the big bang or whatever else is the seedbed of the universe, but with room for development in different directions, especially once life has evolved. In that case God would not directly cause the system of life with its pain and other evils; instead, he brings into being an organic, creative cosmos with freedom built into its very foundations, because without freedom (and consciousness) there cannot be love or creativity, the highest levels of creaturely well-being, which a perfect God would want to foster. But inevitably freedom means that diversity will arise, and diversity means such oppositions as hot and cold, moist and dry, fire and ice, which are the physical basis of natural evil. The latter are the price of freedom, and freedom-loving people judge it to be worth paying, high though it is.

Such a variation of the God-hypothesis seems to me capable of carrying or at least not collapsing under the weight of natural evil. Coupled with the force of the argument that the physical universe is too complex to have any great likelihood of being ultimate and the further argument that the sheer, odds-against complexity of nature suggests a divine creator, this variation would be a more plausible theory than orthodox Christian theism (where God's creative work in shaping nature is much more direct) so far as the facts of nature and especially of natural evil are concerned. And because it is capable of accommodating the reality of natural evil, it would also be more plausible than secular naturalism at the present stage of this process of judgment, by virtue of the theistically favourable argument about ultimate reality. But it is not the theism we find in the mainstream of Christianity, and is thus not centrally at issue in this book. However, it does remind us that there is more to the concept of a perfectly loving God than the familiar, orthodox Christian version of it. As for secular naturalism, the existence of excessive natural evil creates no logical problems because it does not clash with anything in that world-view.

So far as the concept of God being evaluated in this book is concerned, the conclusion to be drawn from the findings of the relevant sciences is thus that neither the Christians nor the sceptics win the argument from nature. *The odds-against bias of the universe in favour of intelligent life points more to a God as its source than to nature alone at the present stage of our scientific knowledge – but natural evil is too excessive and pointless to be the work of a God who is perfectly loving and all-powerful.* For other believers who might favour the alternative concept of a God who builds a significant amount of self-creation into the universe, matters are more favourable, and I would judge their position to be somewhat the most persuasive at this stage of our discussion. They have the benefit of the argument from philosophy, fare well in the argument from physics and suffer no setback because of the existence of natural evil, giving them an overall advantage over both mainline Christians and secularists. But they do not represent the mainline of Christianity.

What is the cumulative effect of the debate so far for the two main participants? Christians have a more plausible view of the ultimate reality and a more likely explanation for the immense orderliness, the bias in favour of intelligent life and its great complexity than their secular rivals; but lose a good deal of this advantage because of pointless, excessive natural evil. The fact that scientific cosmology may yet produce a much simpler account of the universe further erodes that advantage, though not to any great extent since it merely expresses a possible development. *Taken together, all of this cumulatively means that there is still a modest advantage to the Christians.*

In other words, if all that existed were a universe as complex and life-biased as ours, with a planet somewhere containing the highly complicated system of life we see around us including all its deeply disturbing evils, plus intelligent beings like ourselves enjoying a measure of freedom, then the existence of an infinite, eternal and perfectly loving God would at the present time explain those facts rather better than any available naturalistic rival, but without any significant advantage. And the more seriously we judge the problem of natural evil, the smaller that advantage becomes, but it remains an advantage because of the much vaster scope of the believer's significant, earlier advantage in the arguments from philosophical and scientific evidence. Cosmic order and complexity exist throughout the entire universe, and the bias towards intelligent life is present in its very foundations as discovered by physics; natural evil on the other hand is a reality – grim though it is – limited, as far we know, to sentient beings on just this planet, though also having its foundations in the basic structures of the big bang. This is a great difference in scope and therefore works, so far as I can judge, to the advantage of the theist.

Judging the Debate

Humanity: product of nature or child of God?

The first question to be settled in connection with the arguments relating to human nature is whether our human ability to comprehend the cosmos, our self-transcending character and our consciousness make the God-hypothesis more likely than a purely naturalistic explanation of those things. Here again the debate seems inconclusive. These facets of human nature are indeed exactly what we would expect if we have a divine creator who loves us and desires our well-being, for he would want there to be intelligent creatures in his universe who could fathom its secrets and sense his invisible presence behind them; he would equip us with the ability to feel restless with the merely temporary forms of worldly fulfilment and seek always for the pearl of great price which gives permanent fulfilment, namely himself; and he would certainly enable us to be aware of all these things, for consciousness is a richer good than mere existence. And there are undoubted problems besetting the attempt to convert all talk about mental events in purely physical terms, making it somewhat problematic, on logical and linguistic grounds, to treat consciousness as no more than a product of material factors, whereas there are no such logical knots in the thread running from consciousness to a spiritual creator, provided this is not turned into a mind-body dualism. That would present us with the problem of how totally dissimilar things could interact, and so lessen the plausibility of the believer's explanation of human consciousness.

These points, taken on their own and without referring to the sceptic's objections, would not of course make the existence of God probable. Even squaring perfectly with something does not prove that it is true. But those points certainly add to its probability on other grounds. They thus have a confirming rather than a verifying effect. We have seen that so far the case for the believer enjoys a slight advantage over its rival. Thus the believer's interpretation of the source of human nature will further increase the probability of the God-hypothesis being true especially if the sceptic's alternative account proves very weak. But there are of course objections to the believer's interpretation of human nature and its probable source, as we saw in chapter 3. If valid these would deny the believer's theory any increased likelihood, and would even decrease its likelihood if they prove particularly unfavourable to the believer.

The objections in question are firstly that the facts of human nature can just as reasonably be explained as the effects of purely natural causes as any theistic explanation, and secondly that the existence of God would make human fulfilment impossible, so contradicting the Christian idea that God alone can ensure our greatest good.

Appealing to modern evolutionary theory, sceptics say that a being as vulnerable physically as we are could never have survived without evolving the ability to understand the world and its many hidden menaces and its many equally hidden sources of support, like safe foods. This is certainly correct so far as the immediate, physical environment is concerned. But humanity's quest for knowledge is much richer than that, for it seeks out the mysteries of the furthest galaxies and the most abstract philosophical puzzles, which have no apparent or direct biological value at all. In what way does a mind which wonders why anything exists at all, for example, increase its evolutionary fitness? Thus the sceptic's objection is valid for our ability to fathom the immediate physical environment but loses force when applied to other, remoter aspects of our search for knowledge. Yet they are just as real. This weakens the sceptic's naturalistic account of the human mind, but does not refute it because of the points in the next paragraph.

The sceptics' explanation of our self-transcending ability is based on our human powers of imagination and creative effort, and there is no reason, so far as I can see, for thinking that these could not be entirely natural. For one thing, there is no contradiction in saying that an unrestricted, restless imagination has been evolved in a purely naturalistic way; and for another, we do not know the full scope of nature so we cannot possibly insist that nature, in the form of evolution, could not produce such an imagination. A naturalistic world-view does not require that evolution be regarded as a quest for biological survival and no more, a point which is discussed in much greater detail in my earlier book *Religion and Ultimate Well-Being*.

Furthermore, if as purely natural beings we have evolved the mental ability to imagine endlessly better states of affairs and are driven by our natural sentience to want them, then a naturalistic account of our human drive to transcend existing limitations becomes quite intelligible, and adds to the relative strength of the sceptic's argument. On the other hand, the believer's interpretation of self-transcendence is certainly what one would expect if there is a God. So once again I can see no advantage to either side on the point before us. Each view is plausible.

Much the same verdict also arises when we consider the phenomenon of consciousness. Problems of translating mind-talk into physical expressions reflect more on language and culture than on the nature of reality, and even if genuine, would not on their own make the existence of a God probable. And on a Whiteheadian view of things consciousness can be seen as inherent in nature anyway, though most Whiteheadians are also theists. But once again it must be accepted that if there is a God, he would certainly create a cosmos in which consciousness would occur because of its great intrinsic value. The existence of conscious beings is thus fully consistent with the God-hypothesis. However, because such beings can also be explained naturalistically, there is no increase here in the probability of either of the contending world-views.

More serious for the Christian is the objection that if God exists, supreme human well-being is impossible – which is precisely what theism promises that it alone can deliver. As we saw in chapter 3, this objection is based on the orthodox view that an infinite God knows everything, and therefore knows absolutely every detail about our lives, including our inmost selves where we thought we had true privacy. But how can we mature into true selves, with a healthy sense of identity, in conditions where we never really have a moment to ourselves and can never be more than the much-loved servants of the divine king? If there is an infinite God, even a perfectly loving one, then the best we can seemingly hope for is to exist as his beloved children forever. Compared to him who is glorious and infinite and eternal, the rest of us, being fallible, weak and finite, will always be like chickens around a protective and caring hen, in that memorable biblical image, and the proof of this are the metaphors Christianity so often uses to describe humanity in God's sight – lambs, sheep, chickens, children, servants and other immature or subordinate beings – though there are also others of a more flattering kind as well in the Bible.

It is important to see that this is not an argument against the idea that there is a God. Maybe there is a God; but if so, then we humans and all other beings are forever underlings – cherished, to be sure, but still underlings, belonging to and controlled, ultimately, by a heavenly sovereign or father compared to whom we are very minor beings indeed. Maybe this is in fact the way things are. But problems arise when this situation is described as supremely good. How can a situation in which we are forever underlings whose every thought is intimately known by our overlord, perfectly loving and kindly though he is, leaving us no true privacy, be thought of as truly good, except by people who enjoy being underlings or being so intimately known? In other words, the objection doesn't mean that there is no loving God; it means that once more there is a logical problem in the Christian world-view; logically, the best it can promise for humanity is blissful subordination, and that seems a lesser condition than responsible, autonomous selfhood.

The advantage to the sceptic at this point gets less when we recognize the positive side of this problem of privacy, which is that if theism is true then we need never fear being utterly alone or abandoned because of God's eternal and loving presence. And it further decreases if theists were to adopt the view that not even God knows the inner, creative part of us, for the results of creative choice are uncertain and cannot thus be known in advance by anyone, or that he freely restricts his all-knowing powers for our benefit in this respect. This would leave humankind with at least a core of personal privacy, though it could not change our condition of basic dependence on God. But here too we are dealing with a departure from orthodoxy, so this can hardly help the latter. For mainline Christians the problem of privacy and autonomy remains, but it is a problem affecting the logic of describing as supremely good our position as the children of a perfect God, at least in the eyes of people who have come to regard human autonomy more highly than dependence. This objection does not mean that there is no God. Since that is the issue before us, it follows that neither side in the debate has any real advantage here –

just as we found in connection with the other aspects of human nature.

Taking the arguments in this section together, the verdict from philosophical anthropology is therefore that human nature is such as to fit Christian theism and secular naturalism about equally.

Taking all the arguments considered so far in this chapter, the verdict therefore remains where it was at the previous stage of the judgment, namely only marginally favourable to orthodox Christians in their clash with secularists, the argument about what is ultimate and why the cosmos has such a bias in favour of life and such organic complexity being logically stronger on their side of the debate, the facts of excessive, pointless, natural evil being a serious problem for them, and the other arguments being inconclusive.

So far as I can see, an alternative concept of a God who assigns much greater autonomy to the cosmos than is the case according to traditional doctrine even in its most liberal form, should at this stage continue to be judged more probable than the traditional view, and also somewhat more probable than secular naturalism because it is not harmed by natural evil and enjoys a better verdict on philosophical and scientific grounds. On the other hand the traditional Christian concept of an all-determining God would be the least likely view of all. Perhaps the next argument, based on the existence of religion, will tip the scales significantly one way or the other. Let us see.

Is God the true source of religion?

It is here that we run into the greatest surprise in the debate about God, for it emerges that the full story about religion is easier to square, so far as I can see, with a naturalistic world-view than with the existence of the God believed in by mainline Christians. The problem for them is the important fact that the world's religions contain a highly significant non-theistic section, made up as we have seen of people of great spiritual, moral and intellectual quality who find no sign of a God either in their own deepest experiences or in the world at large. Given their stature, their large numbers and the extremely long history of their world-view, it is most unlikely that we can explain them as deluded or perversely blind to the alleged presence of God. When people of this kind over a period of thousands of years in all sorts of contexts honestly find no trace of a God anywhere, then we have to accept that there are problems with the belief that there really is a God who is present everywhere and whose creative hand can readily be inferred from nature, as St Paul explicitly says in the first chapter of his letter to the Romans. Exactly the same applies to the millions of secularists who also find no trace of a God either in their personal experience or in the world at large.

Given the impressive qualities of these people (which is not the same as saying that every one of them is morally and intellectually admirable) it will obviously not do to dismiss them as blind or bad, wilfully turning their backs on a God whom they know in their hearts is there. Nor will it help Christians to appeal to the idea that unless God reveals himself, we can have no knowledge of him, an idea rejected by Catholicism but quite widely held in some Protestant circles. While this can theoretically explain why some people are convinced that there is a God while others are not, it clearly contradicts the central Christian teaching that God is a perfectly just and loving being. Such a being would obviously desire the best for all alike; how on earth could he then *systematically withold* the supreme gift of his own presence from a sizeable section of his people? In other words, there is an extremely serious moral objection to all appeals by Christians to divine revelation to try to solve this dilemma; Christian ethics clash head-on with Christian doctrine in any attempt to do so, making the attempt manifestly irrational.

As we saw in chapter 3, secularists nowadays can produce a naturalistic explanation of religion with far greater plausibility than the theories of Feuerbach, Marx and Freud, and indeed with significantly fewer logical and factual flaws than its rival Christian explanation. But we do not have to accept such a theory to see that the full set of facts about religion cannot logically be cited in support of Christian theism; that argument is seriously flawed in itself because what it implies clashes with proven facts, namely the existence of non-theistic believers and secularists. For example, if a theory predicts that certain people are ignorant, blind or bad, and we then meet those people and find them to be intelligent, sensitive and good, then that theory has in that respect been refuted and must be modified.

But the problem for the believer is even worse because there does not seem to be any way in which mainline Christianity can modify its ideas about how God has acted in order to explain the existence of non-theistic religions and secularism, without departing radically from orthodox doctrine. The sole alternative to the orthodox view that God revealed himself only (or even mainly) through the Judaeo-Christian tradition – a notion which the churches describe as itself a divinely revealed truth – is the view that God reveals himself equally to all his children without bias or favour, which is already a departure from orthodoxy. But this still leaves mainline Christians with the serious problem of explaining why the various religions received such contradictory divine messages and why secularists seemingly get no messages at all. We have seen that those differences cannot plausibly be explained as the result of stupidity, blindness or wickedness, or any other human shortcoming, so mainline Christians would still be left with the contradiction of saying that a perfect God gave all his children the most precious truth of all in an even-handed way, but somehow, inexplicably, only Christians heard it correctly. Obviously this will not do in the eyes of rational judges; it is manifestly incomplete and inadequate as a theory of religion.

So far as I can see, the story of religion on earth and of secularism will not square with the mainline Christian view about a perfectly just and loving God as the source of religion. Thus the evidence forces us to conclude that orthodox believers are in fact impaled by their doctrines on the prongs of a particularly bad trilemma so far as religion is concerned: if there really is a perfect God as the true cause of religion, then he either left some of his beloved children in the dark when they too needed the light, or he misled them, or he never revealed anything at all, so that all religion is the result of unaided human creativity. The third prong of the trilemma means surrendering to the sceptic's theory of religion, the other two contradict the way any reasonable person would expect an infinite and perfectly loving God to act.

How are we judge this situation? The most serious problem is the traditional church belief in a God who supposedly reveals himself to some but not to others. This view places a very large question mark over its own conviction that such a deity is perfectly loving and just.

Alternatively, if he does exist and is really perfectly loving and just, then the church must be wrong when it teaches that he reveals himself so selectively and unfairly. Also problematic is the further doctrine that God's invisible hand can be detected in nature. We have seen the difficulties arising for this belief from the existence of natural evil. Now there is the further problem of why so many good, intelligent and devout people have found no sign of him in the world at large. So we can see why the full facts about religion cause major doubts to arise not just about the way God is said to act but also about whether the God spoken of by Christians even exists.

As a result, I can see no rational or ethical way of avoiding the verdict that the facts of religion confront Christianity with a second really serious challenge, the first one being natural evil. The most interesting way of trying to meet it that I have found is based on an idea of John Hick's, namely that God does not in fact reveal himself in the usual sense. Instead he so cherishes our freedom that he has created us without the ability to be directly aware of him, for such an awareness would be so vivid and overpowering that we would have no choice but to accept God, which means that there would be no freedom in the act of faith, and thus no virtue. It would bring compulsion in where liberty is needed. So God sets us as free beings in a natural environment where we can grow or wither by our own free choices. And although God is invisibly and lovingly present everywhere, this is not evident to us in order to allow us true freedom to find our own way into life and indeed to him. Neither does nature clearly indicate the existence of its creator, for that too would curtail our freedom. Instead, nature is ambiguous – precisely as we have seen in this chapter.

In a universe where people autonomously and unconsciously model the mysterious on the familiar, it is only to be expected that some of them will form the concept of God for themselves, just as secularists say. But instead of it being a mistaken concept, Hick's type of view implies that it is broadly correct, though our human limitations mean that it could never be 100% accurate and comprehensive. This fits perfectly into the fact that belief in one or more gods or spiritual persons is virtually a cultural universal, and varies considerably among them. At the same time the God-given ambiguity of the cosmos, and the fact (if Hick is correct) that God shields us from any direct or clear awareness of his awesome reality, explains why there are people who honestly see no sign of a God anywhere. They would of course be wrong in deducing that there is no God at all, but their error is fully intelligible and not at all blameworthy – especially when it is fuelled by crudities in the theistic religions, for these would rightly make such non-theists critical of theism. As we unfortunately all know, such crudities do exist.

Some such new form of theism would be much the same as the alternative kind I mentioned earlier in connection with natural evil. It is capable of explaining the full facts about religion and secularism more successfully than established Christian doctrine, provided there is also a much deeper and fuller concept of autonomy throughout the whole of nature (in order to minimize the problem of natural evil), and provided also that there is no disadvantage to non-theists, both religious and secular. After all, they can hardly be penalized for responding honestly to a situation where God himself effectively hides his presence in order that we might be free people. And it is surely of the utmost importance to point out that this kind of thinking is entirely faithful to the central message of Christ about a God of everlasting and perfect love as the ultimate source of all things. On the other hand, this view is certainly a radical departure from other aspects of established church teaching because it rejects the age-old tradition that God in fact actively reveals himself, and especially the idea that this alleged divine revelation is largely or even solely confined to the Judaeo-Christian tradition. But our concern in this book is the rational justification (or lack of it) of orthodox, mainline Christian beliefs about God, not radical revisions of them, however promising they may be in their own right, so we must return from this short digression about alternative theism to our central focus of attention.

Religion on earth is no mere local oddity. It is an extremely widespread and very longstanding reality in all cultures. Part of that reality is religion without God, and there is also the widespread fact of secularism. A world-view which cannot do justice to facts of such magnitude places itself under a very big question-mark indeed, especially if it lacks other, decisive grounds to support it. On the other hand, religion is, so far as we know, found only on this planet, so it is a much more localized phenomenon than the complexity and orderliness of the entire universe. This should make us wary of allowing too much weight to the problem posed by religion for the believer. But it is still a very serious problem. Therefore the appropriate verdict for this part of the process of judgment is that *the existence of impressive, longstanding non-theistic religions and of impressive secularists is a fact which would be unlikely if there really were a deity such as the one believed in by mainline Christians, but is not a serious problem for secularists.*

What about the alternative concept of a God who brings into existence a universe which is capable of evolving on its own in various directions and where God does not act directly in either nature or human history, in order to give people real freedom? How does it fare in relation to the facts about non-theistic religions and secularism? Clearly it fares better than the orthodox Christian view, because there would now be much less reason to question why a perfect God would actively reveal himself to or otherwise aid some of his children but neglect the rest.

But still there are problems, for even in this alternative form of theism the God-orientated religions seem to enjoy an unfair advantage arising ultimately from God's design for the universe. They would now be seen as the natural form of religion because it is natural for people to model the mysterious on the familiar, and especially on the model of the personal. Thus even the early, pre-literate cultures of the world developed a belief in one or more personal gods. The great monotheisms would then be seen as later developments of the same basic idea. And both the earlier and the later forms would then be interpreted as essentially correct in their conviction that the universe depends ultimately on one or more divine beings. There would thus be a natural bias in favour of theism, and indeed in favour of the intuitive thinking of early humanity over the more critical and informed mentality of more recent times – unless it turns out that the most rational position to hold is indeed theism. In that case those atheists and agnostics who rest content with their justified rejection of unsophisticated forms of theism, but never bother to ask whether a more sophisticated theism could indeed be true, have only themselves to blame for not moving from atheism and agnosticism to faith in God. Everything therefore depends on whether a revised, modern form of theism does enjoy greater rational support than its rivals, so we can only settle this matter at the end of the debate.

In view of these points it is not surprising that in his more recent work John Hick has developed a different interpretation of religion, defining the various religions as free, culturally conditioned human responses to a transcendent spiritual reality he calls the Real. The concept of God would then be one of many such responses, none of which is capable, humanly speaking, of being judged better than any other. All would correctly grasp some aspect of the Real, none would grasp it fully. To my mind, this theory of religion is post-theistic rather than theistic, for it seems to give up the attempt to square the full facts about religion with any form of God-centred thinking. Whether it can cope with the facts about secularism is another matter entirely, but is not at issue in this book. What is clear, so far as I can see, is that *even the alternative, liberal Christian version of the concept of God is unable to reconcile its notion of a perfectly loving and infinite deity with the fact that there are many millions of devout, decent, well-informed non-theistic believers in the world, whereas secularists do not have this problem.*

We saw earlier that the evidence of philosophy, physics, biology and anthropology, taken together, is only marginally favourable to Christians, so the unfavourable outcome of the argument about religion must obviously remove that slight advantage. Where does that leave things? In view of the severity of the problem posed by non-theistic religion and secularism for mainline Christians, the question must now be asked whether their position can even be judged as having the same probability as secularism at the present stage of our judgment. When a theory clashes with significant, proven facts, that is invariably taken to mean that the theory cannot be correct as it stands, and it is difficult to see why religious theories should be any exception. In that case I can see no way of avoiding the conclusion that the scales have now tipped against mainline Christian believers. This verdict applies to their belief in a God of love but even more so to their view of how he acts. That it should be the phenomenon of religion which has had this effect is itself food for thought. The more liberal, alternative kind of theism we have also occasionally been discussing fares better than its older Christian cousin, of course, but still loses ground against secular naturalism because it too clashes with the facts about religion, though much less severely than mainline theism. All things considered at the present stage of our discussion, I would therefore judge it to have lost its earlier advantage over secular naturalism, but still to have about the same credibility as that rival.

God and human goodness

The facts at issue in the argument about the goodness of Christians and the saintliness of some of them pointing to a perfect God as their most likely source are these: within the churches there are countless people of very great moral stature, noted especially for their compassion and sense of justice. Some of them are indeed moral saints. Secondly, within the same church members there is also much that is not very moral at all, like Christian sexism, racism, economic exploitation and bigotry. Thirdly, a similar blend of goodness and badness occurs outside Christianity, also among secularists.

These facts make it clear that there is not much case for arguing from the goodness of many Christians to the existence of the God they believe in. Such a God may exist, but clearly that cannot be seen from the full facts about religion and morality. In fact, the evidence gives greater comfort to the sceptic than to the believer, for the following reason. If there really is a perfectly good God who is present everywhere in the way Christians say he is, and if a relationship with him is the only effective way to undergo moral upliftment, then his presence can hardly fail to improve all who welcome him into their lives. Why then do we find other Christians who do welcome him but still persist with racism, sexism and other serious evils? And why are there all those millions of non-Christians whose lives are no less caring and decent but who do not welcome the Christian God into their lives at all? If the Christian argument is correct, then it follows logically that the equivalent goodness of these people stems from profound error in their lives, the error of not being in personal touch with the God revealed by Christ and of favouring other gods, or no god at all. In that case, goodness of life is clearly not evidence that there exists a perfectly good deity and that we must be in touch with him if our lives are to be genuinely moral.

There is no need for us to decide whether we accept the sceptic's explanation of conspicuous sanctity, for even if it proves inadequate, it will still be clear that *the argument by Christians that goodness of life in their ranks gives grounds to support their view of God is a failure.* Like the argument about the facts of religion, it founders on the rocks of hard moral fact on a very large scale. And once again, the effect is a further weakening of the case for the traditional, orthodox Christian believer, because the debaters do not earn a tie over this argument; the believers lose it. Thus the scale tips even more against them. Here too changes would be needed. For example, we could logically say that a loving God desires that goodness of life should be the result of humanity's unaided evolutionary struggle for greater well-being, with understandable ups and downs all over the world and no morally elite group anywhere, least of all because of direct divine help. But that is not our concern in this book, except that I must again draw attention to how radical a change from established Christian doctrine that would be. It implies that God no more directly gives any of his people any special moral strength than he gives any of them special revelations or directly creates any aspect of nature. None of these ideas is widely held in the world's churches, and mostly they are rejected.

If the verdict reached so far is sound, and if the established Christian view of God is to enjoy adequate factual and logical support, then the remaining arguments based on miracles, religious experience and Christ himself will have to emerge as strong enough to tip the scale at least back to an even balance. Can they do this? Let us see.

What about miracles?

In discussing miracles we must distinguish between them as part of the objective evidence produced by Christians, and as events which some believers appear to have actually experienced for themselves. We will come to this second aspect later. The first one holds that there is enough evidence to convince reasonable people who bother to look that miracles do sometimes happen – like sudden healings from inoperable cancer after prayers in the name of Christ, or other events which seem to be beyond known scientific laws and powers. Next, believers say that this evidence, while capable of fitting into other explanations, is more likely to result from the loving power of God in answer to some desperate plea, especially if we already have adequate grounds for thinking that there is a God in the first place.

We must grant that this is a reasonable argument as it stands. But sceptics are justified in making certain objections to it: firstly that the evidence for miracles is too slight to be considered really significant, for most of it is of an informal kind without adequate scientific and medical checks. This is not a denial that miracles ever happen; it is a sober comment on the quality of our evidence. It means that the argument from miracles, considered as objective evidence, can at best have a very slight force. Secondly, even for the few well-evidenced cases that we hear about, a God-based explanation loses at least some of its plausibility if other grounds for believing that he exists are problematical – as they are – given the availability of rival explanations and the small number of such events. Therefore it seems only fair to conclude that the God-based explanation of baffling healings and the like is considerably less plausible than it would be if we had better grounds for theism at this stage than we do. Conversely, if the remaining arguments turn out to be strongly favourable to Christianity, then a God-based explanation would gain in likelihood.

The next objection also brings to light problems for Christians, namely the evidence that miracles also happen outside Christianity. The evidence for them is too good to be dismissed as false, though not better than that for Christian miracles (so far as I can see) and I have already shown that there is nothing to be gained and much to be lost by the idea that other religions' miracles are the work of evil spirits conspiring against God. We need proof that these spirits exist outside the minds of some believers before we can give that theory a second glance, and the plain fact is that we have not been given that proof. But even if we had it, there remains the grave problem of calling demonic things which bring good to the lives of other believers. I for one find such a move incompatible with Christian values, and members of those other faiths find them very offensive. So moral sensitivity forces us to accept a positive view of those non-Christian miracles. Since that is not the logical implication of traditional Christian orthodoxy, it follows that there is something amiss with it on this issue. This in turn detracts further from the mainline case for Christian theism, making it rather less probable than it already was. However, it would not detract from the kind of new wave theism I mentioned above, which does not teach that God performs miracles only within the framework of Christianity – especially if taken together with the point to be made in the next paragraph.

Things are better for the believer concerning the remaining objection voiced against the argument from miracles, namely that the ones cited by believers are too sporadic and modest to square with the idea of a God who loves all of us utterly and longs for our well-being. Sceptics find it particularly worrisome that this alleged deity didn't miraculously wipe out slavery or Nazism or apartheid, acts which are obviously within the powers Christians attribute to him. But I think this is unfair to the believer, because any regular or frequent or massive miracles would do grave harm to the very freedom which much of Christianity correctly sees as essential to God's way of doing things. If we knew that God would bail us out every time our evils became really serious, then there would be little or no incentive for us act responsibly to correct or prevent those evils. It is much more consistent with the alleged nature of God that miracles be rare, unpredictable events, as they indeed are. That contributes to our human growth, and is thus quite consistent with the established Christian view of God at its best. It is also consistent with the alternative theism mentioned above.

These considerations mean that *the argument from miracles as objective evidence does not strengthen the case for Christian theism.* While occasional miracles are what we can logically expect from a loving God, the evidence for them is too patchy within Christianity and too prevalent (relatively speaking) outside it to help the Christian believer. Besides, there are other possible explanations for proven miracles than the power of a deity. Since these are unproven, I do not see that the sceptic's case gains any great advantage from them, and therefore judge that neither side wins this particular argument.

So far we have been judging the argument that miracles provide factual or objective evidence in support of Christian theism. What about their subjective impact? Nobody can deny that this is very real and powerful for those who are involved. Imagine a women dying of cancer, the medical world having done all it can. Imagine a friend telling her about a priest with a gift of healing. Imagine him coming to her bedside, talking to her about trusting the unfailing love of Christ, and then praying that if it be God's will, she be healed, laying his hands on her head as he prays. And imagine the feelings of joy, awe and unutterable gratitude if she then recovers. We would be quite devoid of sensitive understanding not to see that for her especially, the healing would be experienced as the strongest proof of God's power and therefore of his existence.

But would this understandable personal reaction count for very much amongst the rest of us? And how sound would the healed woman's faith be, from an objective point of view? My own verdict is that its value as evidence depends on how strong the case for belief in a God already is, on other grounds. After all, if it seems clear that there are problems with traditional theism (as we have so far found there to be) then the logical response to a healing miracle for which no other explanation is to hand, is to judge theism in the light of that miracle more favourably than we previously thought, but still none too probable because of all the difficulties we have been encountering, and to keep our minds open to other possible explanations, or just say that we don't know the real cause. In short, the strong, personal impact of miracles does not at this point in our discussion add to the probability that the Christian God as conceived of in the church causes them, because the other alleged grounds for believing that such a God exists are none too adequate at this stage.

God, religious experience and nature

There can be no reasonable doubt that many Christians do indeed have deeply impressive experiences in which they are sure that they see Christ or Mary, or feel the direct presence or voice of God or the Holy Spirit. But much the same happens in other religions too, for example the profound sense of the seamlessness of reality that happens during Buddhist meditation. What are we to make of these facts? Could they in fact be rationally accepted as adding to the likelihood that the Christian God really exists? If the evidence consisted of no more than Christian forms of experience, then they would, especially as these experiences are surprisingly common, but not with any great force because sceptics have a plausible explanation of their own, as we saw in chapter 3. But the evidence is of course not limited to Christian forms of religious experience. As we also saw in chapter 3, this fact definitely creates problems for believers because none of their attempts at explaining those other experiences will work. This in turn adds to the likelihood that a naturalistic account, or one coming from another religion, or from new versions of theism, is sounder than the established Christian version. *So I conclude that religious experience is too diverse and too amenable to non-theistic explanations – including religious ones – to provide convincing, objective evidence that there is a God as traditionally conceived by Christians, especially when taken in the context of our cumulative verdict so far.* In fact, the converse seems to be the case.

Once again we find that the facts about other religions cause problems for the traditional Christian world-view. That world-view enjoys greater prior probability for its view of God than secular naturalism; it fits very well into the findings of physics and some important aspects of modern biology, though not at all well with natural evil, and also fits about as well as its secular rival into the key facts about human nature and morality. It is when we confront the facts about other religions and cultures – their impressive spirituality, their moral goodness, their miracles and their religious experiences – that serious problems come to the surface for the traditional Christian believer, because none of those realities is much to be expected in a world ruled over by the Trinitarian God of Christianity who, allegedly, is the sole source of goodness and truth and whose benefical acts are confined to the Judaeo-Christian tradition. How could those realities arise independently of his power? But they have arisen, which logically obliges us to reject the orthodox view of God's saving acts. So we are left having to conclude that not even Christian religious experience, considered as objective evidence, can increase the rational likelihood – somewhat modest as it now seems – that the esablished Christian view of God is correct. *And that means that the scale remains tipped in favour of the sceptic at this point, perhaps even rather more so than before.*

As a result, it would, I think, be a mistake to think that the sense of deep inner certainty produced in Christian believers by their religious experiences can count as extra evidence for mainline theism, even for the people concerned. In general – as we saw in chapter 2 – people have a right to think that what they experience probably is the case, unless they have good reason to think otherwise. Humanity cannot function without heeding its experience, and there is no reason to deny this right to Christians. But the vital point is that trusting our experience is valid only if there are no grounds known to us to think otherwise, as with known optical illusions like mirages. As this discussion shows, Christians do in fact have reason to think again very seriously about their traditional view of God and his supposed actions in history, and that certainly reduces the value of their religious experiences as evidence of the existence of that God, especially the idea that they alone know the truth about him. In short, we have to assess personal experience in the light of all the other evidence and not just on its own or within the confines of a believing community where the sceptic's views are never seriously considered. And when we do so, things look much less convincing than they otherwise would.

This verdict is further justified by the fact of secular experience which I described early in chapter 3. It does seem that the existence of large numbers of competent people who experience no trace whatsoever of a God (or of any other religious power) over long periods is very problematic for Christians. It will not do to invoke demons, bad faith or stupidity to explain the fact away. The evidence must be respected, and it shows us that plenty of very moral, honest, caring people, who are not bigots, simply do not experience anything at all which could plausibly be interpreted as the divine presence. Yet if God really is everywhere present and is as evident as these believers say he is, this should not take place. But it does. And since facts count for more than theories, it is the theory or world-view that can't explain those facts that must be judged unfavourably. On the other hand, the alternative kind of theism I have mentioned previously fares better in regard to secular experience, but still cannot account for it very convincingly, as I explained in the section on religion.

At this stage it is helpful to take stock of the present state of our verdict, now that only one set of facts remains to be judged, namely the facts about Christ. Beginning at the most general level, we found that the Christian story about a single God of perfect and everlasting love who was supremely revealed by, and embodied in, Jesus Christ enjoys greater intrinsic likelihood of being a true account of the ultimate reality than the secularists' idea that the cosmos itself, with its complexities, is the final reality. This of itself does not mean that the existence of such a God is for that reason alone likely, especially as there are even simpler concepts available in the other religions; other grounds are needed if that is to be a valid conclusion.

Such grounds can perhaps be found by looking at certain facts of nature revealed by modern physics and biology. These sciences reveal that our universe (or at least our part of it) seems to go back to a massive, original explosion of energy in which things were structured in the one way among very many others that makes life as we know it on this earth possible. Even if there are many other universes, this fact still calls for explanation because there is an inherent logical problem in any theory of the ultimacy of the complex. The existence of a God would provide such an explanation, giving the believer's hypothesis increased probability. And life itself, in the known period of time since it first evolved on earth, is a phenomenon of mind-boggling complexity. That it could have arisen by means of purely natural, random forces, is, at the present state of our knowledge, very unlikely. But if there is a God then there would be no problem. Thus there is a further rise in the probability that such a God exists, but still, of course, no proof, especially since we cannot rule out the possibility that further scientific discoveries will lead to a satisfactory, naturalistic explanation for nature's complexity.

This provisional conclusion, favourable to Christian theism, loses part and perhaps even quite a lot of its relative likelihood when we take into account the surfeit of pointless natural evil in the world, for we would not logically expect so much violence, pain and ugliness in a world directly designed by the kind of God we are discussing. As a result there is a lessening of credibility for mainline Christian theism, which can as a result claim no more than a slight, overall advantage in the debate up to that point. On the other hand a revised concept of God according to which God creates a self-determining universe is much less pressed than the traditional view to explain natural evil, and does not therefore lose ground to its secularist rival on that account, at least not to any great extent.

The various facts of human nature that we considered did not change the verdict so far reached because here too the debaters have equally plausible explanations of the facts. And although this meant a continued but slight overall advantage to the mainline believer (and even more so for supporters of the alternative concept of God), we have still not heard the kind of strong evidence at that stage which could make it likely that theism is true. Thus the believer's case needs strong arguments in its favour. But when we turned to the facts about religion, morality, miracles and religious experience, we found the opposite happening. Those facts, especially the existence of other impressive religions and of morality, miracles and religious experiences outside Christianity, not to speak of secularism, would be unlikely if what Christians have traditionally said about the Trinitarian God is correct – that he exists as the sole source of goodness and truth, and that knowledge of him is available from both his own self-revelations and from an honest look at nature. But facts they certainly are, rendering that view of God sufficiently problematic to have to be judged less likely to be correct than secularism on the grounds so far considered. By contrast, it emerged that a more liberal, alternative view of God faces significantly fewer problems when confronted with the full range of facts concerning religion, so it fares better than the older, traditional view in relation to secularism. But even so, it still falls short of providing a fully satisfying explanation of the non-theistic religions. Obviously this shortcoming detracts from its credibility.

For its part, secular experience of the absence of anything Godlike also poses problems for any kind of belief that the deity is everywhere and can be seen from nature. If he is, why is he so invisible to so many? Therefore this fact also creates problems for mainline Christians, underlining the verdict so far that established, mainline Christian theism does not have greater likelihood of being true than secularism, and in fact emerges at this stage as a somewhat improbable doctrine on the grounds of evidence and logic. The alternative, liberal version of theism, by contrast, must be judged more favourably as enjoying at this stage a level of probability about the same as that of secularism, or at least very close to it. That is how things stand at present. Only some very impressive facts favouring the traditional Christian concept of God could change this verdict into something more favourable to mainline Christianity. Since the only remaining evidence concerns Jesus of Nazareth, maybe it will win the debate for Christians. That depends on whether the facts really do fit their world-view better than secularism – and indeed any other world-view.

The question therefore is whether those facts, which have changed the course of history, make it more rational to accept that Christ was the unique vehicle of a divine power which very closely or even exactly matches the traditional Christian concept of God, than to interpret him in any other way?

Jesus of Nazareth: nobly human or divinely human?

Let us start by recalling the proven facts about Jesus, based on a judicious assessment of the Gospel sources. These facts are that he existed in the time and place claimed by the Gospels; that at about the age of thirty he began a public ministry of teaching that God was the loving, heavenly Father whose kingdom was at hand, and that he himself, evidently under the title Son of Man, was in some way the special instrument of this God, enjoying exceptional closeness to him. For example, he told certain people their sins were forgiven, something which Jews believed only God could do. This message was accompanied by great compassion for suffering, manifested especially as a remarkable gift of healing. Possibly he had other miraculous powers as well. He gathered a group of close followers around him, his disciples, but also generated a wider public following as well as mounting opposition. This came from religious leaders who understandably found those aspects of his message and his actions which seemed to clash with the Law of Moses offensive and even blasphemous. This opposition culminated in his death by crucifixion at the hands of the Roman authorities. But things did not stop there and his disciples, initially shattered by his death, did not simply return to their former lives. This may be because he rose from the grave, as the Gospels say. Though that seems extremely unlikely in itself, at least to non-Christians, the evidence in favour of the resurrection is surprisingly strong, but still too problematic to be conclusive. In any event, either because of such a rising from the grave, or because they came to see Jesus' death as a victory for his message, values and principles, the disciples were soon spreading a message that Jesus was Lord and that he had not ended in death but had risen. Despite serious persecution, their movement took root and has ultimately grown into the world-wide Christian communion.

One key part of this set of facts calls for special comment, namely the evidence for the resurrection. Clearly a resurrection, in the context of Jesus' life, would be a powerful piece of evidence in favour of Christian theism if it really happened. Just as clearly, the case for the Christian believer needs such a strengthening if it is to be finally judged as rationally justified. Over a period of years I have studied that evidence and my conclusion, as given in chapter 2, is that the evidence is too strong to be dismissed as a fabrication but too problematic to be accepted at face value either. This introduces an inescapable element of uncertainty into the debate, at a very crucial stage, and therefore weakens the believers' case, for clearly their case would be significantly stronger if the resurrection could be proved beyond reasonable doubt.

That said, let me return to the set of facts about Christ, and remind readers that we are assessing two rival interpretations of those facts. On one hand we have Christians who are convinced that the facts make far better sense when seen as the work of the Trinitarian God acting incarnately in Jesus and raising him from death. On the other hand we have all the other views of Jesus – Jews who cannot but see him as a tragic departure from their ancient faith; Muslims who see him as a great prophet but still entirely human; Hindus who see him as one of the great spiritual masters, and secularists who think the facts about him can be quite adequately explained in purely naturalistic terms. It is of course the last of these other, rival views that concerns us most right now. However, in testing the Christian view it is not necessary to prove the other ones correct; if there are internal problems in that Christian view, then – in the light of the results of our verdict so far – that alone would mean that the Christian case still lacked sufficient rational justification. Such a verdict does not mean it is false, of course. But it would mean that traditional Christian theism had not been shown by rational means, on the basis of all the relevant evidence, to be rationally probable in its own right and also more probable than its main rival as discussed in this book.

What all this amounts to is whether the facts about Jesus apart from the resurrection tradition really do quite strongly point towards a God as their cause. In full acceptance and admiration of his deeply moving ethical qualities, his beautiful vision of an everlastingly loving God, his deep, active compassion for those who suffer, his inspiring impact, his truly remarkable courage and the unforgettable dignity of his dying in such horrifyingly brutal conditions which could not dim his loving nature even regarding his tormentors – mindful of all this, we must now ask as sensitively to the faith of Christians as possible whether the evidence about Jesus apart from the resurrection really does point strongly enough towards the God of Christian theism as its probable cause, to the extent even of that deity being embodied in him.

Difficult though this will be for many believers to accept, it seems clear that the evidence about Jesus, excluding the resurrection, does not point with sufficient strength to the existence of the Christian God to counter the weight of the arguments against the believer. Why should this be so? Because it is well within the unaided powers of humanity to have formed the idea of a God of love and to act lovingly, for we have seen that there are adequately plausible naturalistic explanations of the God-concept and that very high ethical standards are by no means limited to people who open their lives to supposedly divine influences. The moral quality of Jesus' life is indeed, so far as I am concerned, truly great. But none of us knows what the limit is for human moral achievement, or any other achievement, and there have been other figures, inside and outside the various religions, who have reached the mountain tops of moral stature. At what point, if any, are we forced logically to say that moral greatness cannot be a merely human achievement? Because we do not know the limits of human achievement, none of us can logically identify such a point. And notice that Christians do not argue that Mozart must have been divinely guided in order to be the musical prodigy he was, for they recognize in other areas the point I am making. None of this in the least disputes the superb morality to be found in Jesus; what it does is to acknowledge it and then interpret it, so far as any of us honestly can, in the light of evidence and logical reasoning rather than creed or doctrine.

This conclusion about Jesus' deeds and life-style means that the appeal to the miraculous element in the Gospels is extremely important for the mainline believers' argument. The evidence here is however uneven, as we have seen. Most of it concerns the healings Jesus reportedly performed, but here too we saw that healing talents are not necessarily beyond the scope of nature or of non-theistic spiritual powers. The evidence about Jesus doing so-called nature miracles is too patchy to count as part of the proven facts about him. But even if we give Christians the benefit of any doubt here and accepted those alleged nature miracles as proven facts, it is still possible for Hindus, for example, to attribute them to Jesus' own spiritual mastery over nature, and not to a God as defined by Christians. For that matter, secularists can argue that the correct explanation must be sought within nature itself. So long as our scientific knowledge remains incomplete, as it now is, we are simply not in a position to say with any objective assurance just where the limits of nature's powers lie, so this is clearly a reasonable point. For all we know nature may well have forces that certain rare humans tap into in order to control the ordinary workings of nature. Hypnotism appears to be an example. Therefore any miracles Jesus in fact performed, miracles of healing as well as the nature miracles, do not require us to look beyond Jesus himself or nature for their source. And this of course means that even if healings and nature-miracles were in fact performed by Jesus, that in itself would not add to the probability of there being a God who gave him the power to perform them.

On the other hand, it is clearly possible that a God such as the one believed in by Christians was at work there, if other grounds make it at least somewhat probable that such a God exists. So far, those grounds have not been established. Equally, of course, nothing in our investigation so far in this chapter rules the Christian's God-concept out as demonstrably false, but it does make it somewhat improbable because of all those problems posed by natural evil, the other religions and by secular experience.

What about the resurrection? As I pointed out above, the issue here is the evidence, which is too good to be dismissed as mere superstition but also too problematic to settle the argument in favour of faith in God. Put differently, we can say that there is a problem about treating the reports about Jesus rising bodily from the dead as part of the settled facts about him. On the other hand Christians are right when they fault their critics, both religious and secular, for failing to face the available evidence about the resurrection fairly and squarely. The triumphant, open way his disciples acted after his death in defiance of the very authorities who had him killed hardly seems credible if nothing else happened after Jesus' burial.

How then are we to judge these factors? It seems fair to say that the resurrection tradition rests on sufficient evidence to justify the belief that there may well be more to Jesus than purely human and natural powers, and that a personal God who is infinitely loving – as Jesus said he was – could be that extra power. But the problems about the evidence are great enough to stop this from being more than a possibly correct explanation. The philosopher David Hume correctly reminded us that wise people proportion their beliefs to the evidence. (Imagine the injustices that would follow in our courts if we didn't respect this principle, or the fraudulence in our laboratories and the exploitation in our economies.) So far as I can see, the conclusion reached above is required logically by the evidence. It means that the resurrection evidence is too problematic, impressive though it is, to add to the argument the measure of increased probability which believers need. Overall, therefore, it cannot validly be said that a logically convincing case exists for regarding the facts about Christ as indicating with sufficient strength the existence of a God such as the one believed in by mainline Christians. That is by no means the same as saying there is no God of love at all, a God who builds freedom into both nature and humanity, and whose invisible, enabling presence was the focus of Christ's message and example and who is the just and ultimate basis of all goodness, truth and beauty in every culture and every religion. But as I have now repeatedly said, the debate about God is not in the first instance about that concept but about its older, mainline cousin.

This brings us to the sceptic's attack on the salvation aspect of that mainline Christian concept of God – the idea that the Trinitarian God entered history uniquely as Jesus Christ, who is God the Son and the only saviour, and that only those who believe in him or are nourished by his church can be saved. What is to be said about the merits of this attack? Things are complicated here by the lack of an agreed Christian theology. Church people range from a very traditional and conservative insistence on the correctness of the view summarized above, to what could be called liberal universalism – the view that the God spoken of by Christ makes his saving grace freely and fairly available everywhere. Modern Catholic teaching about the 'universal salvific will of God' seems to belong in this latter category, though other aspects of Catholic doctrine are more traditional. In between these extremes is the theology of those who think that the grace of God is given to all but is especially given through Christ.

Bearing this range of views in mind, let us now note the logic of the situation and then apply it to the various Christian understandings of God's supposed way of saving the world. If humanity really was (or is) in danger of being lost eternally, let alone suffering the frightful fate of eternal torment in hell, and if there was no way humans could save themselves, then a perfectly loving God would certainly step in to help them – even if that meant overriding the freedom he gave us when designing the universe. This may make us wonder why he designed a universe in which such a danger could arise, which could only be overcome by overriding one of the fundamental aspects of his own design. But that would be better than us all perishing. The problem is that according to Christian teaching as traditionally interpreted, God steps in to save us in a way which so far can only benefit a minority of those who need his help. Surely an all-powerful God could have found a more effective, fairer lifeline? And then there is the further problem of whether we have enough grounds for thinking that the human predicament was that bad to start with. As we saw in chapter 3, those grounds are wanting. There is no way I can see a God of perfect justice ordaining that people should suffer eternal damnation for at most a lifetime of sin. Schopenhauer's vivid objection to this notion strikes me as entirely sound.

I can see no logical way out here, and on this particular score the rational verdict seems to be that the Christian story of divine salvation, at least if taken at face value and as taught in the more conservative parts of the church, is exceedingly improbable. It seems much more plausible to treat it as a mythic doctrine produced by the early Christians and expressing their sense of the over-riding importance of Jesus, but not a literal truth, and especially not a God-given literal truth – an interpretation which has already gained a lot of ground in some thoughtful Christian circles. So I think the verdict must be that the sceptics have exposed a very serious logical problem in the doctrines of conservative Christians, who tell of a perfectly loving and all-powerful God who is then said to ordain a punishment for sinful humanity that can surely not be fair, and who then provides salvation in a way that cannot be effective for all. Neither act squares with the idea of God's perfection and infinite power. On the other hand, liberal universalists have little or no difficulty here, but are hardly typical of Christianity. As for those in the middle, whose numbers seem to be rising, they still think that God's saving grace is found in its fullness only in Christ because only in him is God said to be personally present. That leaves them just as open to the valid objections of the sceptics as conservative Christians.

As for the criticism that the orthodox doctrine about Christ (namely that he was throughout his entire existence the union of a perfect human nature with a truly divine nature) – that this makes it impossible for that human nature of his to have been genuinely free, and thus not perfect or ideal, and hence not the sort of thing a perfect God would bring about, here too there seems to be a significant problem for believers if that doctrine is taken at face value, as most Christians do. If the physical and human nature of Jesus was from conception onwards the incarnation of God the Son, at what point could Jesus be said to have freely chosen that status? The disturbing question which sceptics make us ask at this point is thus as follows: would a perfectly loving and almighty God really bring about an incarnation of himself – a bodily entry into history – in a way which diminishes rather than maximizes human freedom, at least for the human being called Jesus? I am unable to find an answer to this which would be both convincing and also remain within mainstream Christian teaching, so I am obliged to judge in favour of the sceptic at this point. Perhaps Christians in the doctrinal mainstream of that religion can find a solution, but in the meantime the present verdict has to stand.

Taking the established facts about Jesus of Nazareth as whole, then, two rather different conclusions are therefore equally plausible. Firstly, his message and actions, the pattern of his life, the manner of his death and above all the persistent evidence that something remarkable may indeed have happened after that death, are all consistent with the belief that the driving force in him came ultimately from something beyond his merely human powers and indeed beyond nature – and similarly that the perfectly loving God he himself found so utterly real was that driving power, provided we do not also insist that it operates at the expense of human freedom or to the exclusion or greater benefit of only part of humanity. But, secondly, it is also clear that none of the proven facts about him demands that interpretation either, so there are valid grounds for being open to other interpretations of the life of Jesus, such as the secularist one or a non-theistic, religious view.

Accordingly, the reasonable overall conclusion about Christ is that the settled facts about him do not make the established, Christian concept of God more likely than any other. And that in turn leaves the case for the mainline believer, taken as a whole, without the strengthening it needed in order to emerge as more probably correct than its main rivals, or even as equally probable. Things are however more promising for the alternative kind of theism touched on at various places in this chapter. It is much less vulnerable to the problems of natural evil and the diversity of religions and philosophies than mainline Christian theism, though still not entirely successful in explaining them. Since those problems robbed the mainline Christian concept of God of its initial explanatory advantage over secularism, this alternative concept of God could be judged at the present time as being about as probable as secularism, or at least very close to it.

The deity spoken of in this liberal alternative could plausibly be seen as the generous and patient ground out of which a self-creating, life-orientated cosmos and within it human culture, including all religion, have autonomously evolved. To that extent I conclude there is some considerable justification for my wondering (as explained in chapter 1) whether the attacks on belief in God in modern times are more a sign that theism is ready for growth into a maturer form rather than a sign that it is on its deathbed. But the rules of judgment followed in this book also lead me to conclude that there is neither factual, logical nor moral justification for the seemingly unavoidable exclusivism and elitism of the traditional, mainline view (especially in its conservative forms), involving as it apparently does the worst of problems for any claim to have found the truth, namely moral unworthiness and the self-contradiction of saying in one breath that God loves us all perfectly, and in another that his unsurpassably beneficial action in history is reserved for or mainly given to the fortunate few in a situation where all of humankind is said to need it.

Traditionalist Christians who disparage rational enquiry in favour of a simple trust in authority will not of course be in the least bothered by this verdict. On the other hand those among them who value rational enquiry might see it as an opportunity to test their own convictions as thoroughly as they would the arguments in this book, and perhaps provide us with rational answers to the difficulties in their position for which I have been unable to find solutions from within the terms of mainline Christian belief.

Having come to the end of the various individual arguments we can now return to our earlier, unresolved question whether the evidence is such that a rational person would be led to favour theism, so that there would be no unfair bias against non-theists in the way God made the universe. So far as the traditional Christian view of God is concerned, the answer seems clearly enough to be in the negative. Rational assessment of the available evidence and respect for logicality would not lead open-minded enquirers to theism of that kind. Things are more promising for liberal theists, as we have seen, but still their faith seems not to have better rational justification than a secular world-view. But if there really is a God who intended that there be a universe like ours – in which very many good and thoughtful people justifiably prefer non-theistic world-views to belief in a God, alongside the majority who are theists of one kind or another – then there is no way of avoiding the conclusion that things work to the disadvantage of non-theists through no fault of their own. By using what must then be seen as their God-given minds in a way not matched by some believers they nonetheless find insufficient grounds for thinking that there is a God, whereas somebody who unquestioningly accepts what the churches teach ends up much closer to the truth. That is hardly what we would expect in a universe where God is supposedly the beginning and end of all things and especially of rational creatures. I find it very hard to see how that could be the will of a perfect creator, and therefore feel obliged to conclude that even the alternative, liberal kind of theism we have from time to time considered falls short of providing as plausible an account of religion as is possible on the basis of secular naturalism, on both theoretical and ethical grounds.

To this the reply can of course be made that in a future life beyond the grave everybody will have the chance to come to a knowledge of God. Belief in a life after death is certainly logical for those who already believe in the existence of a perfect God, for he would have the power and the motive to ensure it. But as Swinburne has rightly said, the appeal to a life after death to make theism more rational has the disadvantage of also making it a more complex notion, and that reduces its inherent likelihood. I therefore think this means that there would be no overall gain for the believer who appeals to the idea of immortality to rescue liberal theism from the problem it faces of being unable to show how the existence of secularists and other non-theists squares with the supposed existence of a perfect deity.

Conclusions

It is time to draw things to an end by summarizing the results of the debate. The issue before us has been whether there are adequate rational grounds for believing that an eternal, infinite and perfectly loving God exists or not, a God whom Christians say is Trinitarian in nature, who has revealed himself in the great events and scriptures of the Judaeo-Christian tradition and who entered history as Jesus Christ, the world's only saviour.

On grounds of prior probability such a God is more likely to be the ultimate reality, the bedrock of all things, than the universe itself, more so if this deity is an absolutely simple rather than a Trinitarian God, all other things being equal. Next, such a God would explain the following rather better than any available naturalistic theory: the odds-against bias in favour of intelligent life that is present in the very foundations of the universe, its great orderliness and its complexity, including the immense complexity of living things. This increases the likelihood that such a God exists. But the surfeit of pointless natural evil on this planet is unlikely to be the work of a loving creator, unless he or she brought into being a self-creating, orderly cosmos as the essential basis for freedom and love. This means that such a deity would seldom if ever intervene in the workings of the cosmos. Since Christianity says that God does intervene, it loses rational credibility in the face of natural evil to both secularism and to the concept of a God whose loving, creative power expresses itself in the gift of freedom to the universe, and must therefore at this stage be judged less probably correct than they are.

The most striking aspects of human nature, chiefly our powers of understanding, self-transcendence and consciousness, are much to be expected if there is a loving God, for they are needed if we are to become loving beings ourselves. The plausibility of theism rises further if such a God were to respect the inner privacy which many people sometimes need in order to mature as selves, a view which is however at odds with orthodox Christian doctrine. But secular accounts of human nature can also explain human nature with about the same plausibility, so human nature cannot be said to add to the likelihood that the Christian concept of God is correct, which is at this stage of the discussion rather less than that of the rivals we are considering.

Moreover, a perfect God would not give the blessing of his guidance only to a favoured section of humanity by causing only their religion and not that of other communities. This ethical principle further reduces the credibility of mainline Christian theism, which implies just such a favouring. A secular explanation of religion as something evolved by humanity makes better sense than this, and so does the alternative concept of a God who lets humanity find its own spiritual direction in life. The same holds for the good and evil to be found in all societies including Christianity. They are what a reasonable, ethically sensitive person would expect if there is a freedom-giving God or if there were no God at all, but are a significant problem for belief in a just God who supposedly gives moral power only or mainly to one favoured community, like the church. This factor further reduces the overall likelihood that the God of mainline Christianity exists, but not that of the alternative concept of God.

Occasional, local miracles which help the individuals concerned are logically in keeping with the workings of a loving God, even one who cherishes our freedom so much that he or she does not ordinarily intervene when we are in trouble. But the evidence is too slight and too open to other interpretations to give objective, rational justification of any real importance for believing in the God spoken of by Christians. Reports of personal religious experience are less rare and patchy than reports of miracles. But they are found in most religions and are in keeping with their character and not with Christianity, so they too cannot count as evidence for the mainline Christian concept of God. On the other hand, they can be given a plausible naturalistic explanation and are also to be expected if the alternative concept of God is correct, by being seen as part of humanity's varied spiritual search. So there is still no increase in the likelihood that the mainline form of Christian theism is rationally justified. And this in turn means that the sense of deep, inner assurance felt by Christians, in the form of a sense of Christ's presence, of God's caring hand, or the Holy Spirit's indwelling power, cannot be judged sufficient to justify their concept of God, convincing though these experiences undoubtedly seem to believers.

The last of the arguments given by mainline Christians to justify their view of God is based on the facts about Jesus of Nazareth. A crucial difficulty for believers is the ambivalent state of the biblical evidence that Jesus rose from the dead. Another one is the availability of other explanations both secular and religious of the proven facts about him, which are much more plausible than most Christians appear to recognize. The proven facts reveal a deeply inspiring religious figure, but they do not strongly imply, let alone logically require, the conclusion that a perfectly loving deity was uniquely present in him. In fact, the doctrine that in Christ alone a God of perfect love and justice offers salvation to an imperilled world – provided people believe in him or belong to the church – goes against what many open-minded people could rationally and ethically believe of such a God. On the other hand, Jesus of Nazareth (and other great spiritual leaders all over the world) can without those logical and ethical problems be seen as an inspiring person giving expression to a sense of the universal, invisible presence of an inexhaustibly loving and beautiful divine reality.

In short, what I have been calling alternative Christian theism is significantly more probable than its mainline, orthodox cousin, and is about as probable as secularism. What cannot validly be claimed, therefore, is that the established Christian concept of God is rationally preferable to its secular rival, or equally supported by evidence and rational argument. That is where the debate leads at the present time, so far as I am able to judge.

In reaching this conclusion on the basis of all the available evidence and by means of rules of judgment which Christians themselves endorse, I am of course acutely aware of how vast is the ocean I have tried to chart and how small my ship and her instruments. If other navigators can correct my mapwork, whether in the direction of a more secular world-view, or in the direction of the fabled continent of orthodox Christianity which seems to me to have evaporated into the mists as I end this voyage and return to harbour, I shall gladly exchange my map for theirs. That ocean is doubtless too mysterious to yield all its secrets to one person's fathomings.

Select Bibliography

Ruth Tiffany Barnhouse, *Identity*, Westminster Press, Philadelphia 1984.

David Barash, *Sociobiology: The Whisperings Within*, Souvenir Press 1980.

Charles Daniel Batson, and W. Larry Ventis, *The Religious Experience: A Social-Psychological Perspective*, Oxford University Press, New York 1982.

Otto Betz, *What Do We Know About Jesus?*, SCM Press 1968.

Colin Brown, *Miracles and the Critical mind*, Wm. B. Eerdmans, Grand Rapids 1984.

Vincent Brummer, *Theology and Philosophical Enquiry: An Introduction*, Macmillan 1981.

Alan Bullock, *The Humanist Tradition in the West*, Thames & Hudson 1985.

David B. Burrell, *Aquinas: God and Action*, Routledge & Kegan Paul 1979.

Humphrey Carpenter, *Jesus*, Oxford University Press 1980.

Arthur C. Clarke, 'The Sentinel' in *Expedition to Earth*, Pan Books 1966.

John B. Cobb Jr., *Beyond Dialogue: Towards a Mutual Transformation of Christianity and Buddhism*, Fortress Press, Philadelphia 1982.

John B. Cobb Jr., *A Christian Natural Theology*, Westminister Press, Philadelphia 1965.

F.C. Coplestone, *Aquinas*, Penguin 1970.

Don Cupitt, *Taking Leave of God*, SCM Press and Crossroad, New York 1980.

Don Cupitt, *Life Lines*, SCM Press 1986.

Don Cupitt, *The Long Legged Fly*, SCM Press 1987.

Mary Daly, *Beyond God the Father: Towards a Philosophy of Women's Liberation*, Beacon Press, Boston 1973 and Women's Press 1986.

Paul E. Davies, *God and the New Physics*, Dent 1983.

Richard Dawkins, *The Selfish Gene*, Granada 1978.

C.F. Evans, *Resurrection and the New Testament*, SCM Press 1970.

Ludwig Feuerbach, *The Essence of Christianity*, Harper & Row, New York 1957.

Antony Flew, *God and Philosophy*, Hutchinson 1966.

James Fowler, *Life Maps: Conversations on the Journey of Faith*, Word Books, Waco, Texas 1978.

Henri Frankfort, *Before Philosophy: The Intellectual Adventure of Ancient Man*, Penguin 1971.

Sigmund Freud, *The Future of an Illusion*, Hogarth Press 1928.

Lloyd Geering, *Faith's New Age: A Perspective on Contemporary Religious Change*, Collins 1980.

Lloyd Geering, *Resurrection: A Symbol of Hope*, Hodder & Stoughton 1979.

William Hamilton, 'The Death of God Theologies Today' in *The Christian Scholar*, 48, 1965, p.31

Norwood Russell Hanson, *Perception and Discovery: An Introduction to Scientific Inquiry*, Freeman & Cooper, San Francisco 1969.

Alister Hardy, *The Biology of God: A Scientist's Study of Man the Religious Animal*, Cape 1975.

Alister Hardy, *The Spiritual Nature of Man: A Study of Contemporary Religious Experience*, Clarendon Press 1979.

Stephen Hawking, *A Brief History of Time: From the Big Bang to Black Holes*, Bantam 1988.

David Hay, *Exploring Inner Space: Scientists and Religious Experience*, Penguin 1982.

Richard Hazelett, and Dean Turner, *Benevolent Living: Tracing the Roots of Motivation to God*, Hope Publishing House, Pasadena 1990.

Brian Hebblethwaite. *The Ocean of Truth: A Defence of Objective Theism*, Cambridge University Press 1988.

John Hick, *Evil and the God of Love*, Macmillan 1966; new edn 1985.

John Hick, *Faith and Knowledge*, Macmillan 1967; new edn 1988.

John Hick, *God has Many Names: Britain's New Religious Pluralism*, Macmillan 1980.

John Hick, *An Interpretation of Religion: Human Responses to the Transcendent*, Macmillan 1989.

John Hick and Paul Knitter (eds), *The Myth of Christian Uniqueness*, SCM Press and Orbis Books, Maryknoll 1988.

Arthur Holmes, *All Truth is God's Truth*, Inter-Varsity Press 1979.

David Hume, *Dialogues Concerning Natural Religion*, Hafner, New York 1948.

William James, *The Varieties of Religious Experience: A Study in Human Nature*, Longmans, Green & Co. 1928.

Select Bibliography

David. E. Jenkins, *A Guide to the Debate about God*, Lutterworth Press 1966.

David E. Jenkins, *Living with Questions: Investigations into the Theory and Practice of Belief in God*, SCM Press 1969.

David. E. Jenkins, *Still Living with Questions*, SCM Press 1990.

Ursula King, *Women and Spirituality: Voices of Protest and Promise*, Macmillan 1989.

Paul Knitter, *No Other Name? A Critical Survey of Christian Attitudes Toward the World Religions*, SCM Press and Orbis Books, Maryknoll 1985.

Lawrence Kohlberg, *The Philosophy of Moral Development: Moral Stages and the Idea of Justice*, Harper & Row 1981.

J.S. Kruger, *Metatheism: Early Buddhism and Traditional Christian Theism*, UNISA, Pretoria 1989.

Andrei D. Linde, *Particle Physics and Inflationary Cosmology*, Harwood Academic Publishers, Chur 1989.

J.L. Mackie, *The Miracle of Theism: Arguments for and against the Existence of God*, Clarendon Press 1982.

John Macneill, *The History and Character of Calvinism*, Oxford University Press 1967.

Karl Marx, *On Religion*, arranged and edited with introduction by Saul K. Padover, McGraw-Hill, New York 1972.

Basil Mitchell, *The Justification of Religious Belief*, Macmillan 1973.

J.P. Moreland, and Kai Nielsen, *Does God Exist? The Great Debate*, Thomas Nelson, Nashville 1990.

Frank Morrison, *Who Moved the Stone?*, Faber 1930.

Gerald O'Collins, SJ, *The Easter Jesus*, Darton, Longman & Todd 1973.

Schubert M. Ogden, *Faith and Freedom: Towards a Theology of Liberation*, Christian Journals, Belfast 1979.

Anthony O'Hear, *Experience, Explanation and Faith: An Introduction to the Philosophy of Religion*, Routledge & Kegan Paul 1984.

Blaise Pascal, *Pensées*. Many editions, eg Penguin Classics 1970; Dent Everyman 1973.

Jean Piaget, *The Growth of Logical Thinking from Childhood to Adolesence: An Essay on the Construction of Formal Operational Structures*, Routledge & Kegan Paul 1958.

Alvin Plantinga and Nicholas Wolterstorff, *Faith and Rationality: Reason and Belief in God*, Notre Dame University Press, Indiana 1983.

Gerald Priestland, *The Case Against God*, Collins 1984.

A New Guide to the Debate about God

Martin Prozesky, *Religion and Ultimate Well-Being: An Explanatory Theory*, Macmillan and St Martin's Press, New York 1984.

John A.T. Robinson, *Can we Trust the New Testament?*, Mowbray 1977.

Richard L. Rubenstein, *After Auschwitz: Radical Theology and Contemporary Judaism*, Bobbs Merrill Co., Indianapolis 1966.

Richard L. Rubenstein and John K. Roth, *Approaches to Auschwitz: The Legacy of the Holocaust*, SCM Press and Westminster John Knox 1987.

Rosemary Radford Ruether, *Sexism and God-Talk: Towards a Feminist Theology*, SCM Press and Beacon Press, Boston 1983.

Bertrand Russell, *Why I am Not a Christian*, Allen & Unwin 1975.

Carl Sagan, *Cosmos*, Random House, New York 1980.

Arthur Schopenhauer, *The Essential Schopenhauer*, Unwin 1962.

Wilfred Cantwell Smith, *Faith and Belief*, Princeton University Press 1979.

Jon Stallworthy, *The Apple Barrell. Selected Poems 1955-1963*, Oxford University Press 1974.

Richard Swinburne, *The Existence of God*, revised edition, Clarendon Press 1991. First edition 1979.

James Thrower, *The Alternative Tradition*, Mouton, The Hague 1980.

Geza Vermes, *Jesus the Jew*, SCM Press and Fortress Press 1983.

Keith Ward, *Holding Fast to God: A Reply to Don Cupitt*, SPCK 1982.

Keith Ward, *The Living God*, SPCK 1984.

Keith Ward, *Images of Eternity: Concepts of God in Five Religious Traditions*, Darton, Longman & Todd 1987.

Max Weber, *Max Weber on Capitalism, Bureaucracy and Religion: A Selection of Texts*, edited by S. Andreski, Allen & Unwin 1983.

Steven Weinberg, *The First Three Minutes: A Modern View of the Origin of the Universe*, Deutsch 1977; Fontana 1983.

G.A. Wells, *Did Jesus Exist?*, Pemberton 1986.

A.N. Whitehead, *Process and Reality: An Essay in Cosmology*, Collier-Macmillian, 2nd revd edn 1980.

E.O. Wilson, *Sociobiology: The New Synthesis*, Bellknap Press, Cambridge Mass. 1975.

E.O. Wilson, *On Human Nature*, Harvard University Press 1978.

Ludwig Wittenstein, *Philosophical Investigations*, Blackwell 1953.

Paramahansa Yogananda, *Autobiography of a Yogi*, Rider & Co. 1950.

Index

African culture and religion, 21
Agnosticism, *passim* but see 79
Amidha, Lord, 61
Anti-semitism, 62
Apartheid, 6, 8, 109
Atheism, *passim*, but see 79
Auschwitz, 116

Barnhouse, Ruth Tiffany, 10
Bible, 29 (see also Gospels, New
  Testament, Paul)
Big bang theory, 47ff., 85, 96, 135,
  159 (see also Cosmology,
  Physics)
Biology and theism, 50–3, 98–102,
  136ff., 171
Brahman, 61, 92, 133
Buddhism, 55, 60f., 79, 80, 92,
  104f.

Calvin, John, 22, 78f.
Calvinism, 78
Carpenter, Humphrey, 120
CERN (European Centre for
  Nuclear Research), 78f., 96
Chinese religions, 55, 79, 133
Christian world-view, *passim*, but
  see, 71–5
Clarke, Arthur C., 86

Cobb, John B., Jr., 92
Communism, 5 (see also Marxism)
Confucianism, 79
Confucius, 93
Consciousness and theism, 54, 97,
  102f., 141f., 171
Conspicuous sanctity and theism,
  63f., 112
Coplestone, F. C., 137
Cosmology, 48ff. (see also Big bang
  theory, Physics)
Creation, 23, 136f.
Criteria for assessing arguments,
  11–14, 131f.
Cumulative arguments, 16, 64
Cupitt, Don, 7, 80, 83

Daly, Mary, 109
Democritus, 80

Einstein, Albert, 72
Ellis, John, 97
Environmental pollution, 4, 109
Epicurus, 5, 80
Evangelicals, 114, 167 (see also
  Fundamentalism)
Evil, problem of, 72f., 95, 98–101,
  108f., 116, 135ff. (see also
  Natural evil)

Index

Feminism and religion, 81, 89f., 109
Feuerbach, Ludwig, 57–8, 73, 106
Flew, Antony, 12
Fowler, James, 10
Frankfort, Henri, 88
Freedom, *passim* but see 128f.,
 138f., 167f.
Freud, Sigmund, 57, 59f., 95, 106
Fundamentalism, 29, 114 (see also
 Evangelicals)

Geering, Lloyd, 124
God (alternative liberal view of),
 138f., 145, 148f., 150, 152,
 160f., 168f., 173
God (traditional Christian view of),
 passim but see 21ff., 42, 72f., 97
 (see also Trinity)
Gospels, 27ff., 29–36, 161 (see also
 Bible, New Testament)

Hamilton, William, 82
Hardy, Sir Alister, 67f.
Hay, Ian, 67
Hebblethwaite, Brian, 50, 52f., 83,
 94
Hell, 25, 127
Hick, John, 68, 72, 122, 148f., 151
Hinduism, 3, 21, 55, 61f., 80, 113,
 124
Holmes, Arthur, 11
Holy Spirit, *passim* but see, 20–22
Human nature and theism, 8f.,
 53–5, 102–4, 141–4, 160, 171
Humanism, 71, 80 (see also
 Secularism)
Hume, David, 47, 98, 128

Incarnation, 22, 27ff., 74, 126,
 128f.

Islam, 3, 21, 56, 62, 64, 71, 81, 93,
 113, 133

James, William, 67
Jenkins, David, 2, 7, 23
Jesus Christ, 2, 21f., 24, 27–42, 63,
 74ff., 81, 82, 91, 104, 108,
 118–26, 161–8, 172f.
Judaism, 3, 21, 24, 62, 64, 71, 81,
 93, 113, 133

Kalam argument, 43, 93
Kohlberg, Lawrence, 10
Krishna, Lord, 61
Küng, Hans, 56

Life after death, 24, 170
Linde, Andrei, 96f.
Love (divine) *passim* but see 23, 25f.
Luther, Martin, 24

Mandela, Nelson, 8
Marcus Aurelius, 1
Marx, Karl, 57, 58f., 106
Marxism, 3, 71, 79, 80 (see also
 Communism)
Materialism, 54, 80
Methods used in this book, 9ff.
Miracles and theism, 20f., 34f., 37,
 64–6, 113–17, 121, 153–6, 164,
 172
Mitchell, Basil, 17
Monotheism, *passim* but see 21,
 62f., 81, 91
Morality and theism, 63f., 108–12,
 152f., 172
Moreland, J. P., 46
Moses, 31, 64, 104
Mother Theresa, 64

Index

Muhammad, 56, 62, 113 (see also Islam)

Natural evil and theism, 98–102, 135ff., 149, 159f., 171 (see also Evil)
New Testament, 28, 30, 32–9, 76, 81, 116 (see also Bible, Gospels, Paul)
Nielsen, Kai, 11
Nirvana, 92

Paley, William, 17
Pascal, Blaise, 83, 93
Paul, 31f., 38, 67, 70, 104, 117, 125, 146
Philosophical anthropology and theism, 53–66, 102–4, 141–5
Philosophy and theism, passim but see 42–7, 92–4, 132–4
Physics and theism, 6, 47–50, 94–8, 135f., 159, 171 (see also Big bang theory, CERN, Cosmology)
Piaget, Jean, 10
Plantinga, Alvin, 69
Plomer, William, 24
Pollution, 4, 109
Pontius Pilate, 34
Predestination, 22, 138

Qur'an, 64, 113, 114

Religion and theism, 55–63, 104–8, 145–52, 171
Religious experience and theism, 20, 66–71, 117, 156–8, 172
Resurrection of Christ, 36–42, 124–6, 162, 164f.
Revelation (divine), passim but see 20, 56, 74, 107

Roman Catholicism, 1, 137
Rubenstein, Richard, 116
Russell, Bertrand, 12

Sagan, Carl, 84
Salvation (traditional Christian view of), 126–8, 166f., 172
Schopenhauer, Arthur, 127f.
Science and theism, 135–40 (see also Biology, Physics)
Secularism, passim but see 79f., 81, 83–92, 118, 120ff., 147, 151, 158 (see also Humanism)
Sentience, 87
Shakespeare, William, 15, 101
Smith, Wilfred Cantwell, 55
Sociobiology, 90
Socrates, 93
South Africa, 6, 8
Stallworthy, Jon, 72
St Augustine, 22, 54
Swinburne, Richard, 45, 46, 67, 170

Taoism, 79, 80, 92, 133
Thomas Aquinas, 17, 44, 72, 137
Traditional arguments for theism, 17f.
Trinity, Trinitarian theism, 22, 27, 34, 93, 111, 119, 126, 129, 131f., 157, 160, 162, 171
Turin shroud, 35

Ultimate explanations, 42ff., 92–4, 132–4
Ultimate reality, 42ff., 92ff., 132–4, 171

Weber, Max, 78

Index

Wells, G. A., 33
Whitehead, A. N., 103, 143
Wilson, E. O., 90
Wittgenstein, Ludwig, 122

Women's movement and theism, 81, 89f., 109

Yogananda, Paramahansa, 113